LAUGHTER

Other books by Joyce O. Hertzler

THE HISTORY OF UTOPIAN THOUGHT

THE SOCIAL THOUGHT OF THE ANCIENT CIVILIZATIONS

SOCIETY IN ACTION: A STUDY OF SOCIAL PROCESSES

AMERICAN SOCIAL INSTITUTIONS: A SOCIOLOGICAL ANALYSIS

A SOCIOLOGY OF LANGUAGE

LAUGHTER

A Socio-Scientific Analysis

JOYCE O. HERTZLER

An Exposition-University Book

EXPOSITION PRESS   NEW YORK

EXPOSITION PRESS INC.

50 Jericho Turnpike   Jericho, New York 11753

FIRST EDITION

LIBRARY OF CONGRESS CATALOG CARD NUMBER: 70-126368

0-682-47118-6

CONTENTS

PREFACE

Laughter has been studied by various disciplines. There may be said to be a rather well-developed philosophy, physiology, and psychology of laughter, each concentrating on the analysis of laughter from its own particular viewpoint. But in spite of the social character of laughter, its ubiquity and universality in social relations and situations, its social effects, especially its social potencies and functions, and its contrived uses for social ends, relatively little attention has been paid to it by social scientists, particularly sociologists.

This does not mean that laughter has been ignored as a social phenomenon. From Plato and Aristotle on we have had a parade of prominent and recognized students of laughter among the philosophers, with their theories of its nature. Some of them have touched on its centrality in social life and have provided rather cogent insights and conclusions regarding some of its social functions and other social attributes and utilities.

There has been some small cognizance of laughter by some of the social sciences during the present century. During the first three decades such psychologists and social psychologists as Sully (1902), Sidis (1913), Patrick (1916), Grieg (1923), McDougall (1923), Allport (1924), and Hayworth (1928), and the psychiatrist Freud (1916), took a marked interest in laughter. Sully especially, in his forty-two-page "Laughter in Social Evolution," Chapter IX, of his classic *An Essay on Laughter: Its Forms, Its Causes, Its Development, and Its Values* (1902), indicated a remarkable awareness and appreciation of some important social scientific facts and principles regarding laughter in human society. The social anthropologist Wallis presented the short article "Why Do We Laugh?" in 1922. In sociology Bogardus had a concise but insightful treatment of "Mirthful Attitudes" in his *Fundamentals of Social Psychology* (1924), and Lumley had a remarkably comprehensive chapter on "Laughter" in his *Means of Social Control* (1925). Since then there have been noteworthy treatments of some aspects or aspects of laughter in social life, mainly in the form of articles or parts of books, by the following sociologists, anthropologists, or social psychologists: Omwake (1939), Burma (1946), Smith and Vinacke (1951), Stephenson (1951), Flugel (1954), Coser (1959, 1960, 1966), Goodchilds (1959, 1964), Middleton (1959), Montagu (1960), Cameron (1963), Zijderveld (1968), Berlyne (1969).

Nonetheless, a search utilizing the usual guides and indexes to the literature, and footnotes and bibliographies in published works that might have some bearing on the subject, reveals a paucity of treatments. For example, I have found no books or monographs by sociologists. And among the hundreds of articles appearing annually in the social-science journals, very few are concerned with laughter. I found almost no reference to laughter in the widely used introductory textbooks or the general sociological treatises.

The present work is a venture in socio-gelotology (Gr. *gelan,* "to laugh")—the systematic study of laughter in social life. It is an attempt to make a preliminary and elementary reconnaissance of the social psychological, sociocultural, and societal place and operation of laughter, to point especially to certain outstanding social scientific, especially sociological, characteristics and implications; in effect, to pose certain propositions arranged and classified according to what can be thought of as major analytical aspects of laughter in social life. Such an orientation and analysis brings out into the open many taken-for-granted features of social interaction. It confronts us head on with new dimensions and relevancies of social realities. As the entire study demonstrates it reveals many heretofore unrealized or glossed over or superficially examined aspects of the social behavior of laughing and smiling.

I have drawn on pertinent material from the philosophic classics on laughter. Works on humor and humorists, on wit and the comic, on comedy and satire, have been suggestive and have provided considerable substantive and illustrative material. The present treatment especially includes concepts, examples, principles and conclusions gleaned from the limited number of works of direct social scientific significance referred to above; these have served as hints, stimuli, leads, and guides for the further development of speculations, conceptualizations, and propositions. The greater part of it, however, draws on my independent explorations, my own experiences, observations, analyses, and theoretical conclusions as a professional social scientist for more than a half century. Most of the names of concepts that are stressed, the categorizations resorted to, and the areas of treatment that have been developed are my own. I have sought to pull together these various elements into a somewhat systematic social scientific presentation of laughter in social life.

A caveat should be sounded, however. This study does not provide an exhaustive body of scientifically substantiated data and tested theory. Only a very limited array is available at this stage of the social scientific study of laughter. Furthermore, we have little direct evidence regarding many of the propositions set forth (though several notable exceptions will be indicated); a host of essential and basic researches are needed to fill this gap. Hence much of what is presented is a point of view, an opinion, a strong hunch. Each proposition, however, may be thought of as a cue or even a hypothesis for more detailed as well as more comprehensive empirical research. The study is thus primarily a "think piece" rather than a research report, a tentative approach rather than a definitive treatment.

Some aspects of laughter presented will appear to be direct opposites or refutations or contradictions of others. This is because laughter is a complex phenomenon; it has many facets and is and does many different things, just like that other major agent of expression and communication, language.

The treatment is not intended only for the specialist students of sociology and the related social sciences. It is of direct practical utility to practitioners in public relations, politics and government, mass communications, advertising, public entertainment, organizational management, intergroup, interclass and interracial relations, mental health, and education. Above all, it is for the intellectually sophisticated general reader who is likely to be interested in new information and perspectives regarding the ways of human beings as they, by their laughter, communicate and commune, enjoy, amuse, control, dislike, oppose and hurt, accommodate to, and otherwise influence and manipulate one another.

A rather extensive bibliography is appended. Where only a particular chapter or particular pages of a book or article are of specific relevance, these data are given. The bibliography contains not only all works referred to in the text but others that have contributed to my knowledge of the subject. It is a fairly comprehensive array of available works that throw some measure of light on laughter as a social phenomenon and a social agent.

Footnote usage, reference to books or portions of books, monographs, and articles depended upon for ideas, quotations, and other pertinent data, and the bibliography itself are according to a somewhat modified form of the method recently adopted by the professional sociological and psychological journals. Footnotes are used only for substantive observations, such as qualifications or explanations of ideas or viewpoints, and supplementary or tangential concepts, facts, and sources; but even these are kept to a minimum. Each citation of source is inserted at the appropriate point in the text within parentheses, giving the author's name and the pagination; if the name has been mentioned in the text, only the pagination. Where an author has contributed more than one work the reference gives the year of publication of the specific work in addition. Page numbers are given without "p." or "pp.," and bibliographical listings are entirely in roman type.

INTRODUCTION

I. Laughter: Its Nature and Its Instrumentation

Laughter is a normal charcteristic of every human being. As Rabelais, the great humorist and satirist, put it more than four centuries ago: "To laugh is proper to the man." Furthermore, according to him, the non-laughers—the agelasts—are "men who are in that respect as dead bodies, which, if you prick them, do not bleed" (Meredith, 3).

1. A FUNDAMENTAL HUMAN PHYSICO-PSYCHIC-SOCIAL ACTIVITY

Laughter is not a trivial or frivolous matter, nor is it an activity detached from utilitarian purpose. To laugh is not necessarily an ill-bred, physical display, or a "lapse from the gravity of reason," or "a kind of degradation," or "a momentary lapse from the persistent attitude of seriousness" (Sully, 1, 25). Nor is it a mere physiological or psychological luxury. Laughter is also much more than a respiratory spasm; much more than a feeling response to the funny, whether of person, object, circumstance, or situation; much more than an expression of humor or mirth. It is a fundamental, complicated, many-faceted physico-psychic-social activity. To be sure, each manifestation of laughter in the individual does consist in a perceptible physical performance: a series of convulsive movements of the diaphragm, causing spasmodic expulsions of breath, with jerky sounds, accompanied by movements of the facial muscles. But the definitive feature of the act is "a surge of vital feeling" in the person laughing that operates as a way of manifesting "vital moods" which are a matter of "inner experience" (Langer, 131; Patrick, 125).

As such, laughter is a multifunctional, universally demonstrated, and powerful expressional mechanism, whose content, import, and intent are in most instances readily interpreted by associates. Of special moment, it is a basic factor in human social existence; it is "part of what we do." (Eastman, 1922, 189, 209.)

As will be noted later in detail, laughter plays an intimate and vigorous part in human social relations and has extensive and diverse utility and employment as an agent of social action. Complex personal and social motives and purposes become involved in its occasions. It has numerous profound functional and structural effects on societal systems. Thus, in its different forms and different interpersonal uses it has vast social scientific, especially sociological, implications.

2.   ITS ESSENTIAL NATURE

We are not concerned here with the total work of laughter. In order to understand it as a social phenomenon and as a societal agent, however, we should have a working comprehension of its essential nature and the conditions of its existence and be able to distinguish it from certain other expressional phenomena closely related to it in some of its forms.

As Lumley (260) pointed out, "It [laughter] must be conceived as a very inclusive term for a great variety of expressional modes, all revealing an attitude toward life." Patrick (101) wrote that laughter is of many kinds, that it arises on many and various occasions, and that no single generalization completely covers it.

A strong case can be made out for each of the widely presented and prestigious—one might say classical—theories of laughter; for example, those of Hobbes, Kant, Schopenhauer, Bain, Spencer, Darwin, Sully, Bergson, Sidis, Freud, McDougall, Eastman.[1]

---

[1] For extended historical inventories and critiques of the theories of laughter see Grieg, 225-279; Hayworth, 380-384; Kimmins, 10-52; Monro, 83-231; Piddington, 13-62, 152-221; Seward, 88-119; Swabey, 198-226; Berlyne, 799-807. Piddington especially presents a systematic review, criticism, and summary of the theories of laughter of some fifty-five writers on the subject from the time of Plato to the present century.

In the analysis of laughter, however, it is not a matter of either-or, of abiding by a single theory. Though some theories contradict others, each has some point, especially in some particular type or types of social situations. Most of the theories dovetail, and all contribute to a more meaningful and comprehensive conception of the complex and variegated phenomenon known as laughter.

It is basic in laughter that in its various forms it is a discharge of energy that occurs when human beings are relieved from a state of suspense or strain or tension; or enjoy relaxation from a situation which has caused surprise, shock, or mishap. It is essentially a way of breaking up or dispelling unused energy, of reducing or easing nervous, mental, emotional, and often physical rigidity or imbalance in the individual or the group in different types of situations.

The conditions under which laughter occurs invariably involve some juxtaposition of elements which are instrumentally, logically, or semantically remote from or in sharp contrast with each other. There is a contrasting of two different frames of reference not usually experienced together. Something which would be appropriate in one is mistaken, or misplaced and inappropriate, in relation to the other. There is thus a linking of disparities.

To understand laughter we must know the situational context from which it emerges. As the analytical treatments variously put it much laughter is a response to some breach of the usual or regular or expected order of events. More specifically, using the frequently reappearing terms of the analyst—unavoidably with some overlapping of the concepts—human beings tend to respond with laughter when they are confronted with the incongruous, the contradictory, the inharmonious, the unfitting, the inappropriate, the imperfect or crude; the accidental, the disorderly, or unusual; the unexpected, unaccustomed, or unconventional; the startling, the mischievous, the awkward; the ironical, the ludicrous, the ridiculous, or absurd; the pretentious, inflated, humbug, or masquerading; the eccentric or queer; the clever and exceptional; the exaggerated, the miscarried, or mishappened; the logically incoherent or implausible; the irrational, the nonsensical, the stupid, or idiotic; the monstrous, the indecent, the deformed, the deviate, the grotesque. Laughter may in some instances be an exhilarating release of energy occasioned by escape from the mechanical, inflexible, and monotonous; and be a reaction to confrontation with dull uniformity and slavish conformity, with the overly proper or overly strict; or with the routine, starched, stiff, and stuffy.[2]

Not all laughter, however, is related to the irregular, the incongruous, the maladroit, the ludicrous, the illogical, the unexpected, etcetera. It also appears in other types of situations. Certain kinds of positive situations evoke mirthful laughter: there is the laughter of merriment, of amusement, diversion, joviality, gaiety. Closely related is the laughter of happiness: the laughter of joy and contentment, the response to the congenial, the comforting, the pleasing, the reassuring—the laughter which comes with the fulfillment of hopes and desires. We also laugh occasionally because of the surprise or satisfaction afforded, not by the unexpected but rather by the expected, as when some person suspected of cockiness or stupidity does perform in a cocky or stupid manner. There is also the by no means uncommon laughter of dead seriousness: the laughter of the person confronted with the truth, the undeniably real, the candid, the straightforward, the thing or act or idea or event *as it is,* in a world of pretense and misrepresentation and over or under emphasis. This laughter is caused by the realization that reality is a startling occurrence or existence or that reality when frankly presented produces pleasant surprise.

It is of key significance in inducing or setting off the act of laughing that there is always a punch line, or punch act, or punch concatenation of circumstances that presents to or confronts the potential laughter with the incongruity, or disparity, or unexpectedness, or novelty, or stark reality in the situation and calls for the switch of ideas and expectations. It is something that trips the trap. Fry (147) refers to it as "the hook on which to hang the laugh."

---

[2] See especially Sully, 82-118; Patrick, 97-142; Lumley, 266-269.

3. AN OPERATIONAL ORIENTATION

Before taking up the more strictly social scientific aspects of laughter, let us look at certain background facts regarding the human dispositions involved in laughter, the implementation of laughter as socially and sociologically significant behavior and as a societal instrument. Particularly significant will be some aspects of the creation of laughter: the laughter-producing acts or behavioral forms, the concrete techniques and devices of humor that induce individual and social laughter, and the media of public humor by which laughter is brought to bear on persons and groups and movements for individual and social purposes.

A. Humor as a human disposition is a prolific source of laughter. Many situations that elicit laughter are defined as humorous. Humorousness itself is a human mental and feeling disposition or propensity. In the individual it is a sportive experience of the imagination with respect to a situation. It operates in different types of actual or imagined situations. The particular situation takes a facetious, or droll, or mirthful, or jovial, or jocular, or amusing, or whimsical, or critical, or ludicrous, or sardonic, or satirical turn as the person perceives and responds to one or more of the possible situational characteristics which evoke laughter, just mentioned above. In general the humorous situation is one in which there is "a linking of disparities" (Monro, 235), "a uniting of incongruities" (Willmann, 72). Of special note, there is always the spirit of playfulness—the playful touch—in humor, even if it is intentionally critical or satirical, or an expression of unpleasantness or frustration.

As the person perceives the situation as humorous, he responds with the physico-psychic act or performance of laughter, which is the correlated behavioral effect. Much laughter is thus the accompaniment and manifestation, the expression, the "speech," and the resolution of humor. Whether deliberately presented or arranged or not, a humorous situation is an invitation to laughter.

Humor appears in many guises, enters into many different

social interactions, and has many social psychological and sociological effects.

Much laughter, however, is not humorous. This, to be examined in detail later, is the laughter of attack, of triumph and exultation, of mere gladness, of relief after tension, the laughter of ego defense, of make-believe, fooling, and mimicry.[3]

Closely associated with the humorous, indeed often used synmomyously with it, are the qualities which produce or mediate the witty, the funny, or the comic aspects of a thing or relation or happening or action or expression of ideas. This is brought out in the standard definitions. *Wit* implies the perception or discovery of unexpected or amusing analogies or associations between apparently unrelated things and the ability to depict them cleverly.[4] It is a sort of contest involving intelligence, imagination, and figuring things out (Rapp, 1951: 70). It is also artificed and intentional. Much wit is deliberately created to show off the skill and ingenuity of the actor. The *funny* is something to which, as we observe its farcical or absurd or droll or nonsensical nature, we have peculiar emotional reactions that provoke us to mirth or joviality. The *comic* as an expression of humor is usually concerned with non-serious incidents which are amusing, or with odd or whimsical or foolish characters, as well as with incidents which are ludicrous. It is always of persons or person-like actions or characteristics. The comic is in contrast with the tragic, sad, ominous, terrible, or calamitous phases of life.

B.   As the human actors act humorously or comically toward each other in producing laughter, they engage in greatly varying types of activity. These range from very mild and positive to very severe and negative actions toward the other persons or collectivities involved in the laughter situation. Some may be kindled by the closest friendliness, the deepest affection, and kindliest mutual and reciprocal regard, and produce the gentlest

---

[3] On humor in relation to laughter see Coser, 1960: 81-83; Eastman, 1922: 1-57; Fry; Monro, 20-52, 112-135, 235-256; Willmann; Wolff, Smith, & Murray, 341-343.

[4] Freud (128-142) distinguishes between "harmless wit," "hostile wit," and "obscene wit." On the relationship between laughter and wit see also Gregory, 121-144.

response. There is, however, some element of critical or aggressive action in most laughter relationships. As implied it often partakes of the nature of an attack.

Widely resorted to among the many forms of action, and involving witty, comical or satirical behavior, are banter; clowning; mimicry; descriptive or explanatory exaggeration or minimization (including overstatement and understatement); burlesque and travesty (ludicrous or grotesque imitation; purposeful distortion of actions and conditions of persons); mockery; caricature (deliberate visual or verbal exaggeration of characteristics of persons); farce (resort to mistaken identities, to mistimings); parody (deliberate trivial or comical imitation); disguise; unmasking; satirical actions (resort to sarcasm, irony, innuendo, derision, ridicule, lampooning); slapstick (rough comedy); invective. There is, of course, some overlapping.[5]

C. The actual cultural structural devices for (1) conveying witticisms, comical situations, humorous pleasantries, satirical sallies, and so on; (2) creating the occasion for laughter; and (3) inducing laughter consist mainly of such as jokes; jests and quips; linguistic mistakes, manipulations, and creations (see chap. xvi, sec. 2); wisecracks; anecdotes (often extended jokes and always about people); stories (tall tales); limericks and other nonsense verses and comic rhymes; gags and hoaxes; some epigrams and maxims; even certain physical postures and gestures.[6]

D. Of the laughter-eliciting devices, jokes seem to be the most frequent, general, and universal, doubtless because they more or less epitomize the use of humor. Nonetheless, we have little sociological information about jokes, either theoretical, descriptive, or applied. But certain sociological aspects of the joke both as a technique or process in itself and as a societal instrument can be indicated.

While the content of some may be frivolous, jokes as a type

---

[5] Freud (289-384) has perhaps the most complete discussion of most of these.

[6] For the description and illustration of some 96 devices "which have been accumulating with the ages," "which constitute the basic structure of humor," and are involved in the eliciting of laughter see Esar.

of social phenomenon are by no means sociologically trifling. They are ancient and are widespread among peoples. They grow out of interaction, are about interaction, and have meaning only in the interaction, between human beings. In our own society they seem to be more widely resorted to than any other laughter device, both by persons in their daily relations with each other and by public humorists. This is not incidental or accidental but rests on the nature of the joke, which in turn accounts for its great and versatile utility.

In structure and function the joke is a prepared and patterned contrivance which always forms a comparison—perhaps better, a clash—of some sort by swiftly passing from one association stream involving an object or condition or idea to another. In the process a switch occurs from the usual or accustomed or logical or otherwise expected to the incongruous or contra-logical or otherwise unexpected. This reversal of what is anticipated, this surprise tactic, is expressed in the punch line which is the climax of the joke. The joke thus presents seeming implausibilities and provides the listener with an upset of expectations. It is this surprising upset of the taken-for-granted which creates the humor and brings the laughter response. But the very implausibility points directly and pointedly to some glaringly ludicrous or painfully embarrassing existential reality. Part of the fun of the joke arises from its being, in its development, a kind of duel of wits between the creator or teller and the individual or collective listeners.[7]

The joke is a highly versatile expressional device. In the first place, as Kronenberger (1953: xi) has indicated, much can be said or suggested or left unsaid by a joke: "How frequently a joke can catch, better than a dozen treatises, the essence of a people, a period, an entire civilization. The world's collective wisdom, we might fairly contend, is compressed into its jokes, which are

---

[7] On the nature of the joke as device see Bergson, 96; Eastman, 1922: 58-120; 1936: 41, 280; Esar, 28-29; Fry, 19-20, 32-34, 145, 148, 156; Koestler, 25, 27; Sidis, 189-199, 203-207, 209-230; Zijderveld, 289-295. For four categories of jokes as "deviations from institutionalized meaning structures" see Zijderveld, 295-303.

teeming granaries of human folly and conceit, credulity and presumption." There is little that cannot be depicted by a joke. It allows, indeed invites, the presentation of a wide gamut of situations and conditions; of feelings, emotions, and sentiments; of values, attitudes, and opinions; of objectives and intentions. The realities as well as the absurdities and inconsistencies of almost every type of social situation can be revealed.

In the second place, jokes have high diffusibility. While funny stories and anecdotes share this characteristic, jokes have certain additional enhancing diffusional features in marked degree. They are thus often included in other types of laughter-eliciting devices, such as anecdotes, funny stories, and limericks. Because they are brief and snappy and pointedly direct attention to areas of wide human and social interest and concern, they spread widely, rapidly, and energetically. Also, because of their succinctness, their sharp point, and their high impressibility for most people, they can be remembered and retold by others, often without losing their intent or effect. They are significant as attention catchers largely because they are always on or at the expense of some person, some human type, some group, some common human situation, some reigning convention, some organization, or some institution. Large numbers of people are thus enlisted—curious about the apparent subject of the joke, or participants in the criticism, or possible targets or victims of the joke. Jokes, being more or less formalized, are recognized as intended to produce a humorous effect or wallop; thus they put people on the alert. Dealing with widely known types of social situations, they are more widely applicable and can be more widely conveyed and utilized than, say jests, gags, quips, or wisecracks, which lose their point when removed from the immediate and momentary situation. They have wider appeal and possibly wider comprehensibility among the different levels of intelligence and cultural sophistication than limericks, epigrams, puns, or the varieties of intentional or unintentional linguistic manipulations.

In the third place, jokes have utility far beyond their immediate function as an expression of humor. They can be used for

almost any social end: both for attacking the ways of others and
for defending against attack; for unmasking absurdity and falsity;
for binding both the like believers and like doers and the
separated or diverse; for warming up audiences or others to
whom an appeal is to be made; for criticism of the atypical and
unacceptable; for social control; and as safety valves.

In the fourth place, the joke is an excellent substitute for some
stern and more elaborate action. It can be used in place of
extensive explanation or exposition; in place of direct criticism
or coercive pressure; in place of argument or wrangling. Also,
because the joke technique calls up a playful mood in the target,
it is often less likely to arouse hostility or stubbornness. One can
often say in a joke what cannot be said directly.

E. Most societies have had their professional humorists,
satirists, comedians, jokesters, clowns, and "fools." These have
functioned in the forum and the market place, on the village
green, in the tavern and coffeehouse, in the theater, at the circus,
at the festivals, in the baths, at the court, at public gatherings,
including political assemblies, in the press and wherever written,
printed, or other graphic or plastic humorous art forms have
been presented or displayed.[8]

F. Historically, various media have been used to elicit
laughter from the public and serve the various purposes of
laughter, ranging from drawings and scrawls and writings on
walls and sidewalks to drama, particularly in the form of comedy,
and organized public festivals. In our mass civilization with its
mass media of communication the following are among the more
conspicuous media for conveying both friendly-amusing and
critical-hostile humor to the public: (1) the literary media, especially humorous novels and poems, satirical and ironical essays and
columns, and syndicated columns of jokes; (2) the graphic media,
especially cartoons, drawings, and comic books and comic strips;
(3) plays (comedies), and comic radio and television skits and
programs.

---

[8] The professional laugh-makers of history will be treated at some
length in chap. vii, sec. 4; chap. ix, sec. 3; chap. xii, sec. 12.

G. Laughter is not entirely or even mainly a matter of socially patterned behavioral forms, or of the instituted instrumental techniques and devices, or the specialized human agents, or the organized activities of the public or mass media. These are culturally developed and established artifices and agents for facilitating or producing laughter. However, the great bulk of the laughter that is socially important and effective requires neither an artificed setting nor a stimulant; it does not have to be elicited or channeled. It is everyman responding to recurrent typical laughter-evolving and laughter-utilizing life situations. The laughter emerges naturally, spontaneously, and normally out of the hourly and daily concrete contacts and interactions of human beings with each other in chance meetings on the street, in the home, while going and coming, while on the job, at informal social affairs, and their other routine contacts and occasions. Everyday existence provides the confrontations with incongruity, illogicality, the unexpected, the exaggerated and the shocking, the comic, the amusing, and the pleasant and joyful; it contributes not only most of the occasions and situations but also the stimuli (incitements) and themes for this universal and seemingly innate behavioral reaction.

4. THE DIVERSITY OF LAUGHTER

As can be inferred from our discussion thus far, much of laughter as it relates to the circumstances from which it emerges, the attitudes it indicates and expresses, the forms which it takes, the functions which it performs, and the media through which it operates is quite different from the conceptions popularly associated with it. The humorous is also a different matter than it is usually conceived and interpreted by those uninitiated regarding its nature and function. Humor turns out to have a wide context and diverse application and utility. Much of our humor and wit is not playful, not for fun; not merry or happy; not merely to exhilarate, amuse, entertain, tease, delight, give joy or pleasure, or produce some other non-serious state of mind or being; not friendly or kindly; not solely to reduce monotony or boredom, or provide pleasant relaxation. Humor is also used to depict and point up a serious situation; under some circumstances it may bring results usually associated with tragedy. Much of it is highly purposive, individually and/or socially, though not necessarily consciously planned and produced as such. Especially important, as already noted, it is used both by individuals and by collectivities.

Frequently laughter takes such forms as relief laughter (relief from strain or tension), laughing it off (a performed stupidity or mistake), contest or triumph laughter, hostile or hurt laughter. Much of laughter is dominated by aggressive or derogatory impulses and expresses criticism, contempt, malice. In its satirical forms humor may be sharp, biting, caustic. Even comedy, which is particularly dedicated to laughter, is used to make the human subject or the butt of the comic portrayal undignified, foolish, stupid, even contemptible. Laughter thus is much more than an overt expression of the blithe or gentle or happy or even comic spirit. We laugh for dozens of reasons. But in all of the different situations laughter, whether humorous or not, whether spontaneous or deliberately creative, organized, and purposive, is a significant social act.

Part One

LAUGHTER
AS A SOCIAL PHENOMENON

II. The Human-social Syndrome
of Laughter

"Syndrome" is a medical term referring to symptoms that occur together in a disease. It has come to have a wider usage. In general a syndrome can be said to consist of two or more sets of conditions, things, or features that invariably occur together. Such an interplay of characteristic *human* and *social* elements, occurrences, and relations may be said to prevail with respect to laughter. Indeed, the human and social aspects seem to be inseparable and integral.

1. LAUGHTER IS PECULIARLY HUMAN

True laughter is a phenomenon confined to human beings. As Piddington (78) puts it, it is rooted in the constitution of the human species. In its crucially distinctive forms (as presented in chap. 1, sec. 2) only human beings create the situations that excite it. It occurs only as a human behavior. Its appeal is to human beings, and they alone respond to it. These facts are unimpeachable. There is, however, a species of expressional behavior laughter-like in some respects that is sometimes confused with true human laughter. It definitely lacks most of laughter's essential features. The nature of this so-called laughter will be briefly set forth here to avoid possible confusion later.

A. Piddington (63–78, 85) has called this "simpler" or "lesser" form "elementary laughter." It is said to be found among some animals, especially some monkeys and apes, among normal infants and very young children, and some persons of low-grade intelligence.[1]

---

[1] My presentation of it is largely dependent on Piddington.

As with language, some psychologists claim that there is something like laughter among some animals. Studies of such behavior have appeared in the literature from time to time. Early impetus was given to this contention by Darwin (198–200).[2] Some of the apes and monkeys have facial gestures that resemble the smile, and they make reiterated explosive noises that sound somewhat like certain laughter in human beings. Darwin mentioned as some of the occasions on which such reactions were observed the return of a person to whom the animal was attached, tickling, presentation of food, reconciliation with the keeper after a quarrel, and caressing. The behavior quite obviously expressed pleasure and affection. One occasionally runs into the surmise among animal lovers that some favored dog or cat smiles.

Elementary laughter among infants and very young children has received much more attention. The occasions recorded by the observers as exciting laughter in the infants include especially warm and comfortable condition after feeding, presentation of brightly colored objects, listening to or making more or less musical sounds, sight of parents' faces, tickling, being tossed or swung about, caressing, being played with, watching other children at play, and playing with toys.

The occasions of laughter among persons of low-grade intelligence, as reported by Darwin, included presentation of food, caressing, presentation of bright colors, and sound of music. Piddington (69) has written that the occasions of laughter among idiots correspond fairly well with the analogous occasions among monkeys.

Obviously there is a vast gulf between this elementary laugh behavior and distinctively human laughter. This laugh is confined to responses to physical, muscular, tactual, and affectional stimuli. It brings only a feeling of physiological or sensory satisfaction and well-being. As Piddington notes (73) it is to be explained on biological rather than sociological grounds. It is not remotely on the level of typical human laughter in diversity, complexity, and precision of expressiveness, and it communicates a limited array

---

2 For a critique of his views see Piddington, 67–68.

of messages. Moreover, it is independent of the social psychological and sociocultural conditions which are typical of humankind. Most significantly, there is nothing in these elementary actions or reactions akin to the human intellectualistic response to the comical, witty, ludicrous, gauche, illogical, or deviant which is of the essence of human laughter.

True laughter, like true language, exists only among human beings. As Muggeridge (59) succinctly put it. "It is their laughter that separates men from gorillas."

B. The common-human aspect of laughter is given emphasis by the fact that ethnologists have found no human group that is devoid of laughter. Furthermore, it is a distinguishing characteristic of our species. Man has been defined as the tool-making animal, the religious animal, the speaking animal, the thinking animal. He is also the humorous animal, the animal that laughs. Whitehead wrote in 1743 in his essay *On Ridicule*:

> 'T was said of old, deny it who can,
> The only laughing animal is man.[3]

Man is also the animal that is laughed at by his kind, the principal butt of his own laughter, and the creature that laughs with his kind.

C. Only human affairs are laughable. We laugh at nothing that does not have a human reference. The special variant of humor, the comic, is referred to as being found primarily in people—in their movements, shapes, actions, appearances, habits, characteristic traits (Freud, 302; Grotjahn, 17). No natural phenomenon is laughable. A landscape or a natural collision of stellar bodies or a swirl of leaves will never be laughable. In fact, no creatures, objects, or occurrences in the non-human world are laughable unless they in some way suggest laughable human characteristics, relations, or actions (Sully, 86; Grieg, 72–74; McDougall, 167; Floyd Allport, 257; Lumley, 266). The behavior of animals is sometimes thought ludicrous, but this is because

---

[3] See also Bergson, 3; Koestler, 3.

it is like that of humans; like that of children at play, or like solely human acts such as a dog walking into a classroom, or like that of fools or clowns, or of frustrated persons—the dog chasing his tail and going round and round in circles. Sidis (102–103) has pointed out that things and objects, including animals, are laughed at in proportion as they are personified as "working . . . similar to the human spirit."

2. THE NATURE OF LAUGHTER
AS A SOCIAL PHENOMENON

Laughter is a social phenomenon. It is social in its origin, in its processual occurence, in its functions, and in its effects.

A. Laughter is born of social contacts, has its roots in social situations, and is a peculiarly social activity. As Bergson (7) put it, society is its "natural environment." Another student (Hayworth, 370) of laughter has stated: "It is as deeply implanted in the social fabric of human society as is singing among birds."

Laughter answers to certain fundamental requirements of the common social life. It is questionable whether a human being would laugh at all if he lived in complete isolation from his fellows.

Laughter grows out of and is occasioned by our experience with our fellow men. It is "a prime part of the interaction process" (Coser, 1959: 171; Montagu, 1960: 32). In the different social situations in which it occurs it implies a kind of interchange with other human beings, real or imaginery, and always involves an element of reciprocity. This is so true that a person in the street or in a public conveyance, being without company but laughing loudly or smiling broadly to himself, is suspected by most observers of being mentally disturbed. Laughter also relates those within the contact circle; actually it invites those present to come close (Coser, 1959: 172). In most of its forms it has determinative interactional effects.

The great bulk of the situations that evoke laughter are social. Essentially they are departures, distortions, exaggerations, even violations, of the laws, the conventions, many of the concepts, and in general the normal expectations and established uniformities of the society.

B. Laughter is shared with reverberating effect. In most of its forms laughter must be shared with or directed at other human beings to be individually or collectively satisfying or socially effective as a form of expression. It exists and is prolonged "by reverberating from one to another"; it "appears to stand in need of an echo" (Bergson, 5–6). The importance of this reverberation comes out, for example, in the telling of a joke. No one gets much satisfaction (kick) out of telling a joke to himself. What is necessary is (1) the teller; (2) the subject, which invariably has a human-interest element—persons in humorous situations—that invites the attention of other human beings; and (3) the audience: those who respond with laughter as the punch line is presented, and whose laughter gives the teller a feeling of accomplishment. In general the making of humor is inseparably connected with the urge to impart it.

3. THE INTERPLAY OF HUMAN AND SOCIAL ELEMENTS

A. All evoking devices and techniques involve human actors. Laughter can be deliberately evoked, stimulated, and activated. Many of the sociocultural techniques and devices to produce and augment laughter mentioned in the previous chapter have been important throughout human history. They have had definite functions and effects in interpersonal and intergroup relationships. They have done much to make laughter the effective instrument that it is. The evoking techniques and devices almost without exception involve socially significant acts of human beings, or human characteristics or other features, or human reactions in more or less common situations. Thus jokes are about human beings in humorous situations, usually involving the unexpected or surprising; cartoons relate to some behavior of some individual or group, or some other human social performance usually to be satirized; caricature is the satirical portrayal of a person vis-à-vis the more normal or conventional person in the situation. Comedy is concerned with "comic" behavior in social relationships and is built around human foibles, follies, and fancies. The humorous and comical in general are always found in people—in their movements, their physical and mental features and traits of character, and especially in their social actions. The satirical stories, essays and columns censure culpable dishonesties, stupidities, injustices, performed by persons, groups, or organizations. Puns and punning and the other amusing or startling linguistic manipulations and mishaps may be instances of the non-personal comic, but they consist in the deliberate or accidental incongruous turns given to persons, things, or occurrences by means of verbal and semantic manipulation of the language institution of the society.

B. Human beings are involved in the manifestations of laughter attending all positive or negative social interrelationships. When the laughers laugh *with* each other, whether mirthfully, companionably, joyously, triumphantly, or derisively, they are in positive mutual relationship and enjoy heightened satisfaction from laughing together with others of their collectivity. As human beings laugh with others they feel, though they cannot always be articulate about it, that they are expressing their collective experience as joint participants in a common enterprise. When the laughers laugh *at* or *against* others, the interrelationship may be close, and it most likely is hostile or negative in one aspect or another, but it is social, usually reciprocally social, in nature. Much sociologically significant laughter consists in people laughing together against others.[4]

In general, positive laughter craves company. The joined laughers share the fun, purpose, and effects of laughing with others; particularly do they feel happier, safer, and surer when laughing in company. In its negative expression laughter seeks targets, in most instances victims but fellow human beings nonetheless.

C. The laughter of the solitary individual is still social. The weight of the all-encompassing society as determiner in laughter is further emphasized by this: that when the individual is alone

---

[4] On positive and negative laughter see chap. iv, sec. 5.

and laughs by himself, whether happily, or repressively, or aggressively, he is not only thereby communicating with himself but is engaged in a pseudo-social affair. One part of his personality may be joking with another part, or kidding it. Much of his laughter and smiling reflects reminiscence of some relation—pleasant, unpleasant, antipathetic—with other people; or, on the other hand, the happy recall of a loved one or a happy occasion, or, in contrast, recall of a contact or incident which still excites derision or contempt; or of amusement at some real or imagined social situation; or the critical application of a prevalent behavioral attitude toward himself; or it may consist of the ironic laughter of disdain of self due to the perpetration of some socially regarded stupidity. Even when we laugh *at* ourselves, we take the attitude of others toward us, as these attitudes reflect standard group conceptions of humorous, especially ludicrous, situations.

D. The imbeddedness of laughter in daily social and societal life is further borne out by its being everywhere accepted (unconsciously, in the main), as a normal part of such life. The agelast—the non-laugher—is looked upon as asocial, if not antisocial, and is labeled, probably correctly, as queer, eccentric, misfit, possibly even mentally unbalanced. As Carlyle put it, borrowing the key phrases of Lorenzo about "the man that hath no music in him" in *The Merchant of Venice*: "The man who cannot laugh is not only fit for treasons, stratagems and spoils, but his whole life is already a treason and a stratagem."

4. THE DIFFUSIBILITY OF LAUGHTER; ITS HERD FEATURES

A. Related to the reverbatory nature of laughter is another of its salient characteristics, its high degree of infectiousness. All in contact have the facility of laughter and susceptibility to it. It has universal appeal: "Laugh and the world laughs with you." It spreads readily among people and can become epidemic. Individual inhibitions are swept away in the wave of joined laughter. The spectators drawn into the laughter circle lose their preoccupation with themselves. The joined laughter can have a kind of feedback effect on the individuals involved and stimulate them to ever more laughter. It can extend to and prevail in wide circles and can accumulate in volume and force. Laughable situations are presented which many individuals would not have noticed or appreciated by themselves. One sometimes has the experience of finding oneself participating in the common laughter even if one has entered the group too late to hear the joke. Because of its infectiousness, even neutrals or persons heretofore not involved in the social situation are tempted to join in on the side of the laughers. For example, in some of its aggressive forms, such as laughter to punish "guilty ones" or to lampoon a perpetrator of stupidities, it may even draw in recent friends or partisans of the victim. The laughter of victory spreads through the triumphant collectivity and becomes more and more exultant as it is shared. The laughter of public rejoicing also multiplies and spreads readily.

This infectiousness of laughter makes it socially effective. Because of it, laughter through social contact and intercourse is a prime factor in the extension, magnification, and intensification of social emotion, attitude, belief, and action.

B.   Much laughter is imitative. Some of it also induces unconscious imitation and participation, even though the imitators frequently do not know what they are laughing about. There are many things at which we laugh in large part because others have often laughed at them in our presence.

C.   An important (and little explored) correlate of the contagiousness of laughter is crowd laughter or choral laughter or herd laughter, whether occurring in face-to-face relations or through the mass media. This can be likened to the baying of the pack. Its central feature is the intense pressure which the laughing mob or herd or pack exerts on human beings, not only sucking them in but as a powerful force coercing all within its range to conform to its objectives or commands. To stand out against the laughter of the herd is to be classed with the rejected, and average man cannot endure this. Furthermore, few persons are strong enough to resist joining in the laughter at some person, group, idea, or activity when "everybody's doing it."

D. Conversely, the herd or the group or the mass, especially the size of the group or mass in which the laughter occurs, is a cushioning or buffering or diluting factor in the moral responsibility of the individual laughers regarding what is freely laughed *at* or *about*. In the large group there seems to be more latitude for letting oneself go. As Allport (258) noted, "Men and women in a theatre audience will laugh boisterously at salacious jokes, which, were they in small groups, would cause them mortal embarrassment." If there is guilt it is the guilt of one minuscule unit among the dozens, hundreds, or millions. There is not only strength but also solace in numbers.

As will be noted later, laughter plays an elemental part in the social behavior of almost all individuals and stands out as an activity of profound social importance in all known societies. Society in large measure determines the laughable. In its various forms it manifests itself as a reaction to and as a potent factor in varied and heterogeneous social and cultural conditions and situations.

III. Laughter as Communication

1. LAUGHTER IS A PRE-VERBAL MEDIUM

Laughter is an ancient and elemental medium of expression. It is quite widely maintained that it and its closely related non-verbal forms of expression preceded verbal language as a form and means of communication, possibly by as much as a million years. It also appears long before speech in the development of the human infant. The consensus among a large number of observers seems to be that many babies begin to smile as early as four to six weeks, and laugh shortly later, often around age three months.

2. THE NATURE OF COMMUNICATION

Laughter is significant in social interaction. Social interaction breaks down into a basic situation and an elemental process: namely, contact and communication. By contact we mean the meeting and simultaneous awareness of each other of two or more parties. Contacts of human beings with each other inevitably involve communication; that is, the transfer or exchange of messages. The messages are structurally constituted of signs, signals, or symbols manipulated by human beings, that is, objects, marks, acts, or sounds without meaning or importance in themselves but assigned more or less specific and standard meaning in the particular culture. The message is transmitted from the originator (sender) to the destination or audience (receiver). The essence of the messages is found in the *meanings* they convey from persons to persons. Technically the conveyance process takes the form of stimulus and response. As soon as one party in the contact situation responds in some measure and form to the stimulus of a sender, and meaning is transmitted to a receiver, communication has occurred. Communication is, in brief, a sequence of stimulus, response, and meaning transfer. Usually it is more or less a two-way, and often a many-way or circular, exchange process, as is the interaction in which it is the elemental social technique upon which all other social processes depend. The specific types of messages exchanged in communication consist in such as communing or conferring with others, of notifying them of conditions, of conveying to them feelings, sentiment, attitudes, ideas, and knowledge, of replying to them, or directing or commanding them.

The techniques of communication which the signs and symbols which present the messages are reproduced and transmitted —the message-carriers—include such forms as gestures, pictographic or graphic and plastic or molded representations, and speech, that is, verbal or linguistic media.

3. LAUGHTER IS ALWAYS POTENTIALLY COMMUNICATIVE

Laughter is always potentially a form or manner of communication. By his behavior, the laugher, unconsciously or consciously, can convey a great number and variety of messages to his fellows. Whether the laughter is or is not deliberately intended or resorted to as a communication transaction, it expresses or indicates meanings to listeners or observers. Even the most private laughter, when noticed by others, evidences moods. Furthermore, each act of laughing, as it conveys meaning to those in the contact network, brings some covert or overt response. Much laughter is intentionally communicative.

4. LAUGHTER AS GESTURAL COMMUNICATION

Laughter should be located as a form of significant human action. Basically it is gestural communication. While there is some disagreement over what is included by the term, the preponderant connotation designates as "gesture" only overt symbolic behavior other than the use of words or visual representations. More specifically, according to this contention, gesture is a means of expressing and conveying to others some attitude, feeling state, emotion, or thought by means of silent physical pantomimic postures or movements of the arms, wrists, fingers, and other parts of the body, by manipulation of the facial features, or by non-verbal vocal sounds, or a combination of these. In delineating the nature of laughter as communication our main distinction will be between non-verbal and verbal behavior.

Laughter is a non-verbal expressive act. It is largely confined to non-linguistic vocal and breathing sounds and to the operation of the facial features, often accompanied by physical gesticulations as a show of feelings, attitudes, moods, and interests. These actions functions as signs and signals, and as we will see, in some of their more standard forms, as symbols. In these respects it is somewhat similar as a means of communication to such non-verbal sounds as grunting, growling, sighing, sobbing, weeping and panting, and such non-vocal signals as nudging, snapping the fingers, and applause. Quite generally overlooked is whistling as a vocal but non-verbal form of gesturing, functionally somewhat similar to laughter as a communicative procedure. It too enables the actor(s) to express moods, convey signals of alarm and greeting, and even transmit specific information under certain conditions. Laughter, however, has a far wider communicative scope and greater versatility and specificity than any of these other gestural forms.

It is frequently overlooked that a great proportion of the contacts between human beings which involve the transmission or exchange of meanings are in part supported or supplemented by laughing, or smiling, in place of or in addition to other means of communication.

5. ASPECTS OF GESTURAL COMMUNICATION

Gesturing is not merely a spontaneous expressive act. It functions both as a direct and independent carrier of meanings and as a supplement to and an emphasizer and modifier of words. Much gesturing is intended to be communicative; it purposes to stimulate response in others: to command, to signal, to beckon, to scare, to inform. We realize our dependence on gestures only when their normal use in effecting person-to-person adjustments is interfered with.

6. LAUGHTER COMPARED WITH LANGUAGE

Laughter is of course a less well organized and less sophisticated system of communication than language. Each language is an established and elaborately organized system with the stable configuration, articulation, and relationship of its component elements. It has its essential, regularized, and conventionally used, rules, its accepted and required structural forms or modes of combining its elements, its methods, principles, and instruments of performance, and its precise and widely uniform meanings.

Laughter does not have the paraphernalia of half a million words as symbols, of a systematic syntactic organization of its parts of speech and a precise and extensive lexicon of words, nor does it have the semantic range, precision and detail of expression possible with a verbal language system. Furthermore, its expressional forms are not so fully conventionalized as words and sentences and therefore not so exact and explicit in conveying meanings. Speech also is usually more direct, deliberate, and calculated than any gestures, or at least can be made so.

7. CONVENTIONALIZED AND PATTERNED FORMS

Though less exact and subject to greater variation than language, laughter nevertheless has features and forms that make it an efficient means of communication. This is because in the given culture or subculture at the particular time and place, much of the interpersonal laughter, like most of the other gestural media, tends to develop the form of more or less recognizable and more or less conventionalized and stylized, even stereotyped, expressional forms for different kinds of recurrent interactional situations and for particular communicative objectives. Basically, of course, the gestures are in general quite meaningless until they are connected with the experience and the culture patterns of the particular society, and until all parties involved in the communicative interaction attach the same meanings to the given gesture. Thus the meanings attached to each gesture are culturally defined, and each society has its own system of standard gestures. Also, it is widely observed that an entire people may develop characteristic gestures.

The standardized laughters convey rather widely understood and well substantiated meanings from actor to audience. Thus, beyond rendering instrumental assistance to language, laughter more importantly is in itself often capable of conveying fairly specific and universally intelligible messages. Indeed, it has some of the functional characteristics of a language.

8.   LAUGHTER AS AN INSTITUTION

Language is an institution, and much laughter, as Floyd Allport (257) long since commented, is "a kind of institution rooted in society itself." Though laughter does not have the full normative and structural organization of an institution, it does have the institutional features of being established in the general social system, of being widely employed by the people of the system, of being more or less uniformly understood in its patterned and established forms, and of carrying conformity sanctions in its use. Like social institutions, it reflects social values, implements social norms, and fulfills individual and social needs. Each type of laughter has its appropriate and peculiar behavioral forms for the different actors in the situation. The laughter for some occasions even has a degree of ritualization (e.g., that between unequals in a hierarchically structured system). Furthermore, the society's laughter in its various standard communicative forms, like other institutionalized behavior, must be learned by the members.

In conclusion, each social system has its large volume of near-institutionalized laughter as well as its "natural" laughter. This laughter has its normative determination of what people laugh about and at, with whom they can laugh, and when they may and may not laugh in different kinds of social situations. Finally, the kind of laughter reflects the kind of communication intended or effected, and most people in the system have little difficulty in ascertaining its particular form, intent, or function. Laughter is a plastic medium and serves a myriad of communicative functions.

IV. The Expressional Forms of Laughter

Laughter is a way of expressing vital moods. As such it can be viewed as (1) an observable physical act, and (2) a form of sociopsychic behavior with vast expressional effect and marked structural and functional societal significance.

1. THE LAUGH AND THE SMILE PHYSICALLY AND EXPRESSIONALLY

The laugh and the smile are both involved in the action that is generally designated as laughter. In general, the two responses are thought of as different degrees of the same human reaction, with the smile physically a weak vestige of the laugh and functionally a lower-key form of the laugh.

The smile and the laugh are different as purely physical acts. Laughter, as already noted, consists chiefly in the spasmodic expulsions of breath, with the quick, jerky, inarticulate sounds, accompanied by characteristic movements of the facial muscles, and brightness of the eyes. The smile is a quieter form of action not giving off sound, and confined to facial gesturing: manipulating the muscles around the eyes and mouth. The grin, with its exposure of the teeth, is an exaggerated smile, a "broad" smile. (Sully, 25–49; Sidis, 1–9; Gregory, 54–55, 155.)

Under certain circumstances, however, the smile can carry as great sociopsychological expressional and communicative force as the laugh. It may reveal a variety of psychic and social psychic states of the individual. It may be a pleased or amused expression of the face. It may manifest joy or pleasure; smugness, approval, indulgence, pity, or affection; suppressed mirth, embarrassment, incredulity, or surprise. But it may also show triumph, sarcasm, derision, disdain, contempt, scorn, or hate. Even small children are able to interpret the smiles of others; for example, whether the smiler is friendly or hostile, indifferent or sympathetic. The smile thus communicates in and by itself. Of equal consequence, it is also widely resorted to as a supplemental or reinforcing complement of verbal communications.

The decibels of sound discharged by the laugher are not always a reliable indication of the expressional potency of his reaction; a smile may often be more decisive and forceful.

Several operational aspects of the smile should be noted. Many individuals who would be conscious of the physical act of laughing because of the expenditure of energy involved are frequently unconscious of their act of smiling, which in many situations may be quietly spontaneous and almost reflexive. Thus, not infrequently, they are unintentionally but visibly revealing to others their attitudes of amusement, their feelings of friendliness, or of antagonism or contempt. If the observer can observe the immediate spontaneous smile expression of the smiler before he wipes it off or dresses it according to the conventions, he often gets a more true and accurate response of the person—even a confirmation of his attitude at the moment. There is also, of course, the simulated smile used to lie and betray, as well as for control, especially to stimulate response. The simulated sneer-smile may also be used to convey an insult or to show contempt.

For our purposes, except where the distinction is specifically indicated, we shall consider smiling a form of laughing.

Physically there may be many laughters. They may range from the faintest or gentlest smile, through the broad smile, through moderate laughter, to the uproarious, explosive, almost uncontrollable physical upheaval of the person (Darwin, 208). A classic description of laughter at its peak of physical exuberance is that of Carlyle in *Sartor Resartus* (Book I, chap. iv) when he vividly presents the response of Professor Teufelsdröckh to the proposal for a "Cast-metal King":

Gradually a light kindled in our Professor's eyes and face, a beaming, mantling, loveliest light; through those murky features, a radiant ever-young Apollo looked; and he burst forth like the neighing of all Tatersall's,—tears streaming down his cheeks, pipe held aloft, foot clutched into the air, —loud, long-continuing, uncontrollable; a laugh not of the face and diaphragm only, but of the whole man from head to heels.

The laugher may merely smile soundlessly; he may chuckle, giggle, titter, snicker, or cackle; he may crow or guffaw; he may howl the house down.

2.   EXPRESSIONAL STATES CONVEYED BY LAUGHTER

Our main concern with laughter is that as it is involved in the interactions of two or more persons, it is a widely understood and widely employed way of communicating. More specifically, it reveals various kinds of individual and social states to others, and is a way of attracting attention, of informing, declaring, conveying attitude and opinion, and of eliciting reactions from others. Concretely, there are many varieties of laughter—almost as many as the stimulus conditions. The range is astonishing. Many different classifications are possible and fruitful, depending upon the analytical aims or the pragmatic concerns of the classifier. It is most appropriate early in a sociological consideration of laughter to view it in its different personal and interpersonal expressional manifestations. We thus present a general classification on the basis of the form of the act of laughing among others— laughter as a social behavior.

A.   In some of its forms laughter is mainly a way of individual expression of inner states that may or may not be socially caused or conditioned, but expressions which are not in their nature necessarily shared with others, and do not have socially declarative intent or have other people as partisans or targets. However, the sociological signicance of such self-expressive laughter lies in its usually being readily interpreted by associates or other persons aware of the laughter; it reveals the individual physical, psychic, social-psychic, or social state, tone, and posture of the person at the time. Such laughter has a wide range: (1) the quiet smile or the gentle purring laughter of contentment and inner peace; (2) the individual laughter of relief or escape from physical or mental pain, or from depression, suppression, or oppression; (3) the smile or laughter of self-assurance; (4) the laughter of delight or mirthfulness; (5) the laughter of amusement; (6) the "happy laughter": the chuckle or chortle of gaiety as an expression of cheerfulness, good humor—"the joy of the merry heart"; (7) the laughter of exhilaration and high spirits; (8) the laughter attending physical vitality or exuberance; (9) the subdued laughter of embarrassment; (10) the laughter of surprise; (11) the laughter at an actual or imagined funny idea, act, or situation; (12) the laughter of incredulity; (13) the laughter of nervousness; (14) the laughter of self-consciousness; (15) the laughter of extroversion; (16) the laughter of sardonic emotion.

What might be correctly referred to as social laughter can be classified respectively as laughter *with* other individuals or groups, and laughter *to* and *at* or *against* others. These forms of laughter are profusely used and have profound social effects. They overlap somewhat in particular instances.

B. Laughter *with* others takes various forms: (1) the bubbling laughter of sheer playfulness, lightheartedness, and mutual pleasantness with associates in congenial social situations; (2) the laughter of amiability, agreeability, friendliness, emotional warmth, and reciprocal genial feeling; (3) the joined laughter of amusement; (4) the joined laughter that breaks down barriers; (5) the laughter that is attractive and invitational; (6) the hilarious, uproarious, gusty belly laughter of shared humor and mirthfulness of a crowd; (7) the more or less surreptitious and not infrequently derisive and malevolent laughing or smiling used in gossip with others about another or others not present or not included in the immediate group of associates.

C. Laughing *to* others is a way of conveying information about self or group or about an existent social situation to other persons, and laughing *at* others, with the exception of one form, is malicious and intended to be humiliating, a show of hostility—hurtful, punitive, or destructive.

In laughing to others we have such forms as (1) the loud high-pitched cackle of the showoff or attention-drawer; (2) the laughter of friendly greeting or of welcoming others; (3) the laughter of encouragement to others; (4) the laughter of approval and applause; (5) the laughter of sympathy and empathy; (6) the laughter of self-defense among others; (7) the veiled laughter of warning; (8) the gentle laughter of friendliness, tenderness, affection, or high regard; (9) the laughter of intentional insult; (10) the laughter to frighten others; (11) the laughter of defiance; (12) the taunting grin ("Do it if you can!"); (13) the laughter that signals social safety.

Laughter *against* or *at* others takes such forms as (1) the laughter publicly expressing for all within range self or group congratulation, self or group superiority, pride, conceit, approval; (2) the exultant laughter of successfully unmasking the opponent or disliked person or group; (3) the stentorian "thrashing laughter" of triumph, victory and conquest; (4) the satirical laughter of disapprobation, of criticism, of censure—the "blow in the face" laughter; (5) the raucous laughter of vituperation, derision, ridicule; (6) the insidious sneering laughter of contempt, scorn, and abhorrence; (7) the laughter of malignity and malevolence; (8) the laughter of rebuke; (9) the laughter of bitterness; (10) the laughter of sarcasm; (11) the laughter of rejection, repulsion and exclusion; (12) the sly snicker or snigger of disbelief.

3. AGGRESSIVE AND SUPPRESSIVE LAUGHTER

Most of the laughter directed *against* or *at* others falls under the very general categories frequently found in the more or less socially conscious treatments of laughter; namely, (1) aggressive laughter: the laughter of antipathy, antagonism and attack, the laughter directed at or against other individuals or groups, or what they stand for or do or have done, in order to control them, exclude them, reject them, humiliate them, weaken or injure them, punish them, defeat them, and, in some instances, destroy them; and (2) suppresive laughter: the laughter due to the atmosphere of constraint, restraint, taboo; the laughter directed against the social suppressor, the oppressive authorities, the conventions, many features of social institutions, the majorities, the totalitarians, the jailers, the dominators, the "superiors." (Freud, 138-142, 153-161; Patrick, 106-110; Rapp, 1949: 81-96 and 1951: 109-131.) Suppressive laughter is, in the main, the laughter of the underdogs, the "outlaws," those absolutistically controlled by tyrants and dictators, the oppressed majorities, or unequally treated minorities. It is the laughter which gives the laughers a rebound, or a rescue, or a freeing from a feeling of suppression; it is for them an expression of victory over the repressors. (See chap. xii.)

4. NON-PURPOSIVE AND PURPOSIVE LAUGHTER

A second contrasting of laughter forms, already implied, is that between socially non-purposive and purposive laughter. Non-purposive laughter appears more or less spontaneously and is engaged in without specific intentional objective. This is the laughter of relaxation, release, joy, amusement, gaiety, friendly feeling, and other expressions indicated in section 2A above. Purposive laughter is employed deliberately and designedly to approve, reprove, disapprove, unify, warn, encourage, command, deride, humiliate, insult, or condemn others (section 2C above).

5. SOCIALLY POSITIVE AND NEGATIVE LAUGHTER

Another fundamental dichotomy of laughter is that between socially positive and socially negative laughter. This rests upon the quality of contribution the laughter makes in the promotion or retardation of social values. Social values, as estimates of social worth, affect the social intentions of people, and are exemplified in the social and societal effects of their action. Every individual or social act of the socius is placed on an evaluational scale.

A major distinction is that between positive values, which

relate to what is necessary, advantageous, worthwhile or desirable, and negative values, which are concerned with what is disadvantageous, undesirable, harmful, destructive. With respect to laughter as influential social action this is paralleled by positive and negative laughter.

Positive laughter is beneficial laughter—laughter that reflects the positive social values and contributes to the affirmative and constructive ends and purposes of individuals, or groups, or categories of persons, or the community or society. It is altruistic and makes for what is socially good, desirable, ideal. Not only does it have alleviative and restorative capability and effect, but it is conducive to general individual social health and well-being and to the advancement of the social systems in which it occurs and has its effects. It can also be a potent propulsive factor in social well-being.

Negative laughter is socially harmful or destructive laughter; it has anti-social effects. It leads to the misfiring of social purposes, and brings about social contradiction, negation, denial, loss, depreciation, deterioration, demoralization. In general, it redounds to individual and social dysfunctioning. When it is intentionally perpetrated, the purpose is to impugn, confound, defeat, injure, or destroy the target.

V. The Sociocultural Context of Laughter and Its Themes

Laughter is not an indiscriminate response, and nothing is laughable in itself. The laughable is what particular persons or groups laugh about or at. The laughers, however, do not laugh in a simple, single, uniform, unchanging, sociocultural environment. Their respective social milieus present a variety of settings and numerous variables in the forms of historical cultural deposits and contemporary constituent elements and social situations. These different types of social situations invite different types of laughter, that is, different types as forms of expression relating to and resulting from the situation, and different types to meet varying functions and objectives in the different types of situations. Furthermore, the same situations do not necessarily elicit similar response from all people of the given social situation; individual differentials exist.

Thus an important aspect of laughter as a social phenomenon is that in its different guises it grows out of and reflects its different sociocultural contexts. It always needs a subject, and it always is linked to a situation. The culture of the society, the more permanent groups to which the laughers belong, the nature of the occasion, the territorial location, and the time or era in the flow of sociocultural change in considerable measure establish the grooves of awareness, interest, concern and intent, set the subjects of what is laughable, and thus supply the relevant stimuli for laughter. In brief, each culture (or nation), each group and collectivity or population segment, each locality (area or region), each occasion or type of interaction, each age or era (even each moment), has its peculiar laughter themes. Many of these themes involve hidden references known only to the members. Therefore, since laughter is essentially what men make it, it is necessary, in order to understand it, to observe it and know it in its particular social and cultural environment at each given time and place.

If laughter is a sort of language, then there are many different laughter "languages," and within the languages, dialects, special group and interest-area jargons and argots, and other "special-isms."

The different elements of and relations in the context will be briefly examined. There will be some overlapping, however: the elements are not mutually exclusive.

1. THE CULTURE (OR NATION) AS CONDITIONER

Cultural conditions in general greatly influence laughter. Each culture sets the subjects of major interest and concern. It has its own distinctive social, economic, political and intellectual history; its own fundamental values; its own distinctive social codes— folkways, mores, manners, customs, conventions, and laws; its own battery of positions and roles; its own logic; its own ideology; its own *Weltanschauung,* that is, its own attitudes toward different aspects of the world and of life; its own body of sentiments; its own semantic system; its own image of itself vis-à-vis other cultures; and, above all, its own peculiar complex of social institutions in large part setting the behavior patterns of its people in almost every department of life.

Each nation, as a culture and a going societal concern, has a somewhat distinctive character and spirit in contrast to other nations; distinctive and peculiar in the sense that the elements which enter into the character and spirit are much more common within the particular nation than anywhere else. This accounts for the considerable similarity in the actions of the individual members in most typical and recurrent social situations. The fact is also borne out by the differences revealed by a comparison of the national characters of the English, French, Italians, Germans, Russians, and Americans, such as Martindale's (1960: 7–22). The national culture that produces the national chaarcter puts its stamp on its people as individuals and as groups. It rules and shapes their ideas and reactions and produces a set of typical and distinctive behaviors. Even in a highly diversified society like our own, the various subcultures—within communities, regions, social classes, occupational groups, even ethnic groups—reflect the over-all national configuration of characteristics.

Of special moment, the features of the national culture and character are reflected in the nation's humor and laughter. This native, or national, quality of humor was recognized more than a hundred and thirty years ago—

> Humor . . . is impregnated with the convictions, customs, and associations of a nation. . . . The humor of a people is their institutions, laws, customs, manners, habits, characters, convictions,—their scenery whether of the sea, the city, or the hills—expressed in the language of the ludicrous. . . .[1]

These culture elements (1) provide much of the background and base for the laughter of the people; (2) contribute the subject matter—the nation's peculiar laughter themes and forms; (3) establish or greatly influence what it is permissible to laugh about or at and what is tabooed, and whom to laugh with and when. As an example of peculiar laughter themes and conditions, the political conditions in a nation may markedly affect the types of humor and laughter in vogue, the types and themes induced, tabooed, or permitted; notably in a democratic as against a totalitarian nation.[2]

An important social psychological aspect of this national-cultural setting for laughter is that the individuals are born into it, live their lives in it, or enter its all-pervasive influence as immi-

---

[1] Quoted by Blair (3) from *Westminster Review* (London), Dec. 1838.

[2] On national differences in humor see Kimmins, 126-166; Eysenck; Smith & Vinacke; Rourke. As an instance of the determinative influence of the over-all setting see the essay by Rovit on the effect of American life on Jewish humor, including that dispensed by the many professional Jewish humorists.

grants. Much of their laughter thus is due to the particular laughter stimuli in the sociocultural environment which set it off as conditioned response. The established features determine the content and thrust of the stimuli as they in turn set off and give impulse to the reigning laughter forms and emphases. They have this effect during the entire lifelong socialization of the individuals.[3]

The choice of many of the subjects of laughter is nationally conditioned. This affects everyday humor and laughter. Thus much of the humor of other contemporary peoples does not seem to be very funny. Many Americans, for example, are unable to get much of a kick out of some of the jokes or cartoons in *Punch* or *Simplicissimus,* or those now translated from *Pravda.*

Proverbially, a person cannot laugh heartily in a strange country.

2. GROUPS, COLLECTIVITIES, SUBCULTURES: AUDIENCE DIFFERENTIALS

Each group, each collectivity, each subculture, in addition to having the general determinants of culture or nation as a whole, has its special variations of the national culture. This simply means that each also sees the world from its own special point of view. Hence, each also has its own peculiar laughter themes, awareness of the laughable, and causes of laughter. Likewise, much laughter is confined to the particular group; often one

---

[3] The part of laughter as a medium of communication points to the basic significance of the common nation-wide or society-wide culture. Communication denotes the presence of a number of essential common factors. It cannot take place without these. If there is to be an effective communicative exchange, with adequate conveyance of meaning the participants must have a common fund and a common level of sufficiently uniform experience. They must possess uniform patterns of awareness and attitudes, similar responses to given standard types of stimuli, a certain amount of understanding, agreement, and shared knowledge as to common aims and values. The more these conditions prevail the more universal and uniform will be the behavior patterns within the social system, including the patterns of laughter.

group will laugh at or about a given situation, and another will not. Non-group members sometimes cannot or will not (because of the contra-group situation) laugh with members of other particular groups. It reminds one of Bergson's account (6) of weeping: "A man who was once asked why he did not weep at a sermon when everybody else was shedding tears replied: 'I don't belong to the parish.'"

Each group, collectivity, or combination of people in a given situation constitutes an audience; and each audience has its own peculiar receptivity to laughter stimuli, and its own variations of laughter. The same joke or comic situation which convulses one audience meets with indifference or even disapproval and hisses from another.

Subcultures vary in what they laugh at and about. The background of knowledge, the educational level, the degree of cultural sophistication, and the intellectual habits of the people as individuals and as particular cultural groups, are very important factors in differentials in laughter. Mention need only be made of the people who are inspired to laugh at jokes in the *New Yorker* and those who "read" the pulp comics.

The identifying diversions of given occupational collectivities differ. For example, each occupation and profession has its own brand of humor. What a group of college professors laugh at, a businessmen's group may very likely not. Soldiers have an extensive array of laugh specials. Many musicians' jokes are hardly comprehensible to non-musicians. A plumber's joke with another plumber about a repair call may provide uproarious laughter for them but be considered insulting by the housewife concerned.[4]

Each age group (notably teen-agers), each ideological group (notably communists as against non-communists), has its own brands of humor and its own laughter themes. The different national and ethnic social groups (Scottish, Irish, Jewish, Italian, German, Negro, Spanish-American) have their peculiar types of humor (Barron; Middleton & Moland).

---

[4] On the determinative effect of occupational experience see also chap. vi, sec. 3D.

Laughter occurs under peculiar conditions in special audiences. As an example, in a night club we have a favorable social poise for laughter on the part of the patrons; the general atmosphere is one of complete relaxation and sometimes of abandon. There is a strong element of safety in the semi-darkness; hence, there may be jokes of a quality that would not be used (or at least laughed at) if the laughers had spotlights on them. The crowding (usually sought by the operators) creates the moral relaxation and the submergence of self-consciousness that comes with crowd squeeze. Finally, the alcoholic state of much of the clientele loosens physical and nervous tensions and moral restraints, impairs judgment, and causes greater subjectivity to mental absurdities and stupidities.

The different status groups, including social classes and status levels in all manner of organizations, have their subjects and codes of laughter as affected by hierarchical structure, power-authority differentials, system of role allocations, and so on. Variations in religion, economic interests and level, political interest and affiliation, and other societal and cultural identifications have their own peculiar accompanying laughter.

3. THE OCCASION

It has been indicated above that laughter frequently is only in part "genuine" or "natural," that is, a spontaneous discharge of nervous energy that has suddenly become redundant. Much of it is forced, artificial or conventional; in other words, a voluntary, or habit-conditioned redirection of laughter-energy to fit it to the type of social occasion. The occasion may more or less dictate the importance of a particular kind of laughter and thus create a sociocultural pressure to laugh. There is, indeed, what might be called protocol laughter. This is the artificed and usually more or less stereotyped, or even ritualized, laughter that the social situation with its special type of relationship of the interactors requires; for example, the tooled-up laughing by well-bred guests at the joke or other witticisms or attempted droll antics of the host at a dinner party, or the laughter by subordinates at the humorous sallies of their organizational or other social superiors. Similar is the laughter decreed by etiquette or good form for the occasion; for example, the goodwill smiling of the public official when he addresses his constituency, or the carefully contoured smiles exchanged in the line at a formal reception.

The themes also differ with the type of occasion. The jokes the minister uses in his sermon are quite different in subject, tone, and color from those told by the night-club entertainer. Inappropriate laughter in a serious situation may complicate it or nullify it as a positive or fruitful interaction. The Moroccans have a proverb: "Laughter cancels the sale."[5]

Not laughing in certain situations conveys certain implications; for example, in a group of people laughing together, the non-laugher may be thought either stupid or a social rebel, and most people seek to avoid such labels.

Though not sociocultural factors, the social-emotional state and the spirit of the group has some effect on its laughter. Jokes and stories are usually funnier when told in high-spirited company; general merriment often carries off a mediocre jest.

4. THE LOCALITY

Locality affects what people laugh about. Basic in locality is the physical environment as a determinant with marked cultural implications and effects. The physico-geographic regions—each with its special global location, its peculiar terrain, climate, weather, native and domesticated fauna and flora, natural resources, characteristic economic and occupational conditions, its population elements, and its natural hazards—affect every person and group, and every department of life of the communities of these regions. Jokes and humorous stories involving physiographic features, weather, typical seasonal occurrences, native animals, indigenous or typical people, level of cultural sophistication regarding the different regions of the United States have characterized some of our choicest humorous writing—Mark

---

[5] On other types and subjects of themes and their fitness or unfitness for particular types of circumstances and occasions see also chap. xv, sec. 3C.

Twain and the Mississippi, the tall tales of Davy Crockett's pranks, the whoppers about Paul Bunyan. John Steinbeck's *Travels with Charley* is a current example.

The ruralites, the villagers, and the city folk have their own laughter themes; and they laugh at each other. Londoners laugh about many things that Parisians do not. Europeans laugh about many things that Africans do not, and so with American mid-westerners and New Englanders.

A good many laughter items are so local in meaning that they are not at all amusing to outsiders, sometimes even when explained or translated.

5. THE TIME AND ERA

Each particular time, each era, in fact each moment, has its own conditions and themes for laughter—its own run of attention—because of the major preoccupations, concerns, interests, activities, relations, and modes prevailing at the time. This means that there is a weighty element of topicality-temporality in the laughter of people, an element that reflects the affairs of the day and era, and changes from day to day and era to era.

Looking back in time in man's career, we see that much of what is laughable has varied with each stage of civilization. Even a span of only a few centuries shows marked changes in the definitions of humor, and a comparison of peoples of different stages in culture presents marked differences in the materials which cause laughter among them. Stage of civilization, of course, involves level of knowledge, of ethical viewpoints, of technology, and social structure. As will be noted later there have been major differences in the different stages of cultural development in humanitarian viewpoints as they affected laughable conditions and subjects. And you cannot produce mirth by referring to left-handed monkey wrenches if the technology is that of the Paleolithic.

As times change, what is respectably funny also changes. The good jokes of one age are not necessarily good in another age. The more universal laughter themes are not static. In recent times among us, and reflected in the jokes, have been changing attitudes toward sex; new, more liberal attitudes and less interest in religion; new, more realistic attitudes toward natural functions. In general, jokes and other laughables are related to and compatible with the temper, occurrences, and concerns of the given locale and time. Whatever holds the attention of many at the moment is likely to be joked about. And these laughables change with circumstances, and with changing attitudes, values, and interests.

Historically the very situations that induce laughter at one time may disappear and be replaced by others as changes occur in the social life of a people. In the United States we have had a succession of humor-laughter themes. The march across the country and the settling of the West during the nineteenth century produced its spate of jokes and its singling out of hunters, frontiersmen, and backwoodsmen as comic types. The gold rush had its own rush of humor. After the Civil War when city people became aware of ruralities and during the struggle for power between rural and urban Americans (1875–1925) much laughter was occasioned by jokes about the country rubes or bumpkins, hayseeds, and clodhoppers. The rural sympathizers, of course, countered with jokes about city slickers and city smart-alecks. Today, with around 70 per cent of the population living in metropolitan areas, relatively few persons are involved in rural or small-town life, and hick jokes have practically disappeared.

During the period of approximately 1850–1914 when immigrants came in great numbers, they were the subject of a flood of jokes. With the marked reduction of immigration after World War I, such jokes began to decline, and now there are none. The Pat and Mike jokes died out long before one Irish immigrant's son ran for the presidency and another attained it.

Each of our wars has produced its special humor, reflecting climate and geography of the location of the personnel, the special characteristics of the enemy, the type of warfare, and so on. When Negroes became a sizable and conspicuous minority, or when there has been abundant racial contact, then "race" jokes have proliferated. Dialect jokes have flourished where and when dialects have confronted each other, and with the weakening of dialects in many parts of the country have almost disappeared. We had prohibition jokes only during the prohibition era.

In the twentieth century we have had such laughter-eliciting characters as the well-meaning but distraught common man, the self-made man, the rugged individualist, the mass-man, and especially the social climbers and status seekers. At the present time jokes abound about traffic conditions, hippies, and yippies. Cold-war jokes and space-age jokes are common.[6]

Quite understandably, the nature and subject matter of suppressive laughter—the laughter against social restraints and restrainers—has varied from age to age in communities and societies as each age's shoe pinched in different places.

Another aspect of the place-time factor relates to the weight of the contemporary mores in determining what you should and should not laugh at, in the light of the momentary standards of decency and chivalry. There are also always vogue and fad themes of the moment: what is fashionable or "in" as humorous or ludicrous. Likewise, the mores change with time. What is a pleasant or amusing peccadillo in one era may in another become a matter of honor and death. The conception of what constitutes breaches of the social order changes; what is fitting or congruous at one time is unfitting or incongruous at another.

It is also obvious that some moments are more propitious than others. When a person makes a joke or tries to be funny at the wrong time or on the wrong occasion, people laugh at him rather than with him, or even damn him as uncouth.

It may be concluded, then, that the "going laughter" of any "going concern" has occasion fit, place fit, and time fit.

6. LAUGHTER AS SOCIAL INDEX AND COMMENTARY

In general, laughter serves as a kind of sociocultural index of the culture or society, the groups and population segments, the

---

[6] On American humor as a demonstration of the time factor see Blair; Winick, 1961; Yates.

communities or localities, and the eras in which it occurs. In an article, "We Are What We Joke About," in the September 5, 1939, New York *Times* Magazine, the great Canadian humorist Stephen Leacock declared: "Let me hear the jokes of a nation and I will tell you what the people are like, how they are getting on and what is going to happen to them." More recently the sociologist Middleton (175) stated: "There is more than a little truth in the maxim of the field anthropologist that when the investigator has progressed to the point of understanding the jokes of the native people as much as half of the time, it is possible for him to leave the field confident in the knowledge that he has a thorough understanding of the basic elements of the culture."

What a people laugh at at any given time can reveal what they perceive socially, what they are interested in, concerned about, amused by, disgusted with, preoccupied with. It reflects their current tastes, thoughts, and sympathies. Laughing at given opinions, beliefs, codes, etiquette forms, and so on, means that the members of the group or society, or some considerable part of it, are conscious of their contemporary foolishness, archaic nature, freakishness, inadequacy. When the community laughs with the assistance of such concrete devices as jokes, satirical columns, and cartoons, at values, mores, or institutions, or personages, or organizations, or other social relations, structures, or affairs, it is revealing bad spots or sick spots; it is pointing to what seems to it to be unfitting, anti-social, vicious, uncouth, or otherwise faulty. Thus the laughter is often a pertinent commentary on the fundamental judgment of the community. For example, the fundamental values of a people stand out in their laughter-inducing media, as is seen in the United States. Stephenson (574) noted that many of our jokes reveal "an adherence to a set of values regarded as the traditional American creed." To refer to the sociological conceptual category of stratification, for instance, the jokes tend to minimize stratal differences and to "maximize the expression of American values as embodied in concepts of equality, ambition, initiative, opportunity, enterprise and the like" (Stephenson, 574).

The laughter of others at our group may bring us illuminating glimpses of ourselves as others see us, and thus also provide us with valuations of ourselves and possibly guidelines for behavioral revision.

It is obvious, in the light of the above, that the subject-matter content of the laugh media, particularly the jests and jokes, and the comedies, cartoons, and satirical pieces, when examined for given periods of time, throw much light on the values, standards, and institutions—the general state of affairs—at different moments in the past.

Changes in laughter habits or themes are a moving index of the course of social events and attitudes; they reflect the movements of the civilization of a people. Gregory (9-19), for example, calls attention to the marked changes in the "humanity" of laughter subjects. The period A.D. 1561-1679 was an inhumane one by our present standards, and could be said to be a period of inhumane laughter. The objects of gleeful laughter were such as deformity, infirmity, and cripples. Now such laughter is tabooed as inhumane.[7]

It is appropriate here to call attention to the valuable public service rendered by many of our public humorists. First, the themes these humorists present are both a topical index of and a comic or satirical commentary on the most pertinent interests, tastes, social conditions and problems, events, and personages of the given time. Second, they do this in an especially effective manner because of the peculiar nature of the media they employ. The public humorists—whether by literary means (witty or satirical essay or column, syndicated joke column), pictorial means (cartoon, pictorial caricature, comic strip), or radio or television or motion-picture comedy or skit—through their comic and usually critical presentations of reality as they see it, can make people understand and feel things they never could expect to understand or feel in reading the soberly and objectively presented facts and opinions in the prose of the newspapers, magazines, governmental reports, and so on. They give concrete details in

---

[7] On laughter as index see Gregory, 84-99; Duncan, 1953: 51-52, 55; Duncan, 1962: 398-490! Hall, xiii-xiv.

attention-catching and readily comprehensible form. They appeal because the characteristics and details of the situations they depict come right out of the experience of the average man. They report realistically on human life, and are a force against superficiality, subterfuge, flimflam, glossing over. They demonstrate that truth can be portrayed covertly, subtly, and effectively from behind the comic mask. They have always been a national asset.

Incidentally our American public humorists as they have presented our different ethnic and racial elements, our dissenting minorities, our current character types, our regional values, attitudes, and ways, our dialects, our diverse and often conflicting interests, and so on, have reflected our demographic and regional diversity, our pluralistic culture, and our cosmopolitan character.[8]

7. UNIVERSALS VERSUS SINGULARITIES; BARRIERS AND ISOGLOSSES; NON-TRANSLATABILITY

The discussion of the present chapter points to certain other related facts of distinct sociological significance regarding certain sociocultural aspects of laughter. The first has to do with universals as against singularities in the laughter themes of cultures and collectivities. The distinctive individuality that we have noted which in some measure marks the laughter themes of each populaton segment, each group, each region, each era, each country, should not obscure the fact that there also are universals in laughter. There are some common or recurrent laughable situations that go back to the primitives and the ancients. According to Eysenck (1945: 332), many contemporary jokes in representative German, French, English, Danish, Norwegian, American, Italian, and Russian journals are surprisingly similar.

There are bound to be many situational, relational, and contextual uniformities in human society. People everywhere have a number of similar perennial subjects of hilarity, such as insults,

---

[8] For a more extensive treatment of American public humorists, with special stress on their function as social critics and controllers, see chap. ix, sec. 4.

sex, vanity, masqueraders and pompous persons, matrimonial relations, bad manners, scatological acts, foreigners, sometimes categories of persons, such as priests and preachers or teachers (Sully, 82–118).

Ancient themes may reappear in a new guise. Many jokes are contemporary applications of ancient themes or are concerned with ludicrous aspects of universal situations or are old patterns somewhat refurbished to apply to the present. Cameron (98) has aptly termed such jokes "re-treads." He mentions that old military jokes are reissued with each war (reflecting new conditions, personnel, enemy, materiel, etc.), and some drunk jokes have been rerun as narcotic jokes and beatnik jokes.

Each nation and each culture also has its broad band of common and more or less durable laughing themes over and above the more singularistic ones of particular groups and sections that are related to the salient and more characteristic features of the culture. In the United States we have such stereotyped themes as husband-and-wife relations, adolescent behavior, drunks, the foibles of our statesmen, our overdogs, status seekers, status symbols, social climbing, smog, women's clothes, women's efforts to conceal their ages, and regional weather.

The sociocultural singularities of laughter, as the converse of the more universal features, are of equal importance. The vast proportion of these singularities are as likely to continue as are the infinitely diverse determinative conditions that call them into being.

Singularities are illuminated in part by certain ecological aspects of laughter. Owing to differences in themes between nations (as geographically defined entities) and communities, and also because many themes are confined to particular collectivities having specific locality, many forms and themes of laughter have more or less determinable physical extent and boundaries. In fact, it would seem that the social ecologist could draw isoglosses of laughter areas and boundaries similar to those devised by dialect linguists. The ecological factor explains why laughter often balks at regional boundaries or national frontiers.

Another piece of evidence supporting the singularity of the

given body of humor is that much that is humorous or otherwise laughable for one culture or nation cannot be accurately
and exactly translated into humor and laughter for another, or
often even readily interpreted. This non-translatability has two
closely related aspects. The first grows out of the fact that the
language of each society and community is somewhat unique in
its structure. Languages have some non-parallel lexical, syntactical, and semantic elements that greatly retard or confuse
direct translation.[9]

The second, and broader, sociocultural-contextual aspect of
the non-transferability and self-containment of humor and
laughter is probably even weightier than the linguistic factor.
Owing to the differences in the sociocultural context of humor
established between cultures, nations, groups and collectivities,
regions, and eras, much that is humorous and laughable for one
sociocultural segment is meaningless or even repugnant for
another. The social and cultural experiences are so different,
possibly even non-duplicatable, that the respective people have
differing and non-matching themes. Indeed, one people may
actually completely lack some themes which abound among
another people, so intimately do laughter themes reflect the
subtle and unique as well as the more general features of the
social heritage and the outlook on life of the people. Also, similar
experiences may be considered humorous by one people, and
non-humorous, even serious or stupid, by another. *Pari passu,*
given that similar types of laughter behavior may have very
different meanings in different lands, then conversely, different
laughter gestures may have very similiar meanings. Finally,
differences in laughter patterns are significant deterrents to the
growth of intimacy and understanding between people of different societies, classes, regions, or other social groupings or collectivities.[10]

---

[9] This sociolinguistic factor and its effect on the humor and laughter
of a people will be examined more specifically in chap. xvi, Sec. I, "Sociolinguistic Aspects of Humor and Laughter."

[10] On the non-translatability of humor and laughter see Grieg, 71-73;
Leacock, 83-84, 201-202, 226.

VI. The Subjective Aspects of Laughter

1. WHAT INDIVIDUALS LAUGH ABOUT AND WHY

Various past thinkers in attempting to explain why human beings laugh have largely confined themselves to one or a few types of physiological and psychological reactions to one or more mirth-provoking characteristics or conditions of objects, or persons, or interrelational occurrences among or between these. In total, however, these provocatives of laughter, as indicated by the different analysts mentioned in Chapter I, section 2, have been numerous. It is difficult to select from this array any one all-sufficient guiding principle. As stated earlier, laughter is complex; it is the product of many inducing factors. It is especially significant that different individuals will laugh, or not laugh, for very different reasons under identical conditions. Furthermore, the laughter of an individual is in some measure a response affected by his moods, feelings, attitudes and relational circumstances at a given moment, and may differ at other moments.

What is important in the present study is, first, that the physiological-psychological act of laughing by the individual "laughing animal" in his environmental setting, though variously induced, renders him socio-psychic, therapeutic, and interactional protective and restorative services in varying social situations in which he finds himself. The individual, as individual, laughs for usually discernible reasons.

Second, though laughter is common to and universal among all men, it varies greatly among them as individuals. They have personal characteristics, both inherently and as the result of social conditioning and social opportunity, which affect them differently in given laughter-inducing or laughter-utilizing situations.

Third, because of these factors affecting individuals, the laughter of each person throws much light on him as the particular, peculiar individual that he is.

2.   WHAT LAUGHTER DOES FOR THE SOCIUS

Every individual is a socius, that is, a participant in social relationships or social behavior. Laughter plays a crucial part in the best organization of the personality of the socius and in the daily, even momentary, accommodation of him as a personality to his associates in the different kinds of interactional situations that arise. Furthermore, he laughs because he must in order to live with himself among as well as with his fellows. Nietzsche maintained that "man . . . had to invent laughter to preserve his sanity."

Some of the more obvious services which it performs for the individual follow.

A.   Laughter provides a remedial personal relaxation from tension and suppression. Considerable attention has been paid to laughter in general by the outstanding gelotologists—the students of laughter—as a technique of release and as an easer of tension. There is a marked similarity in their conceptualizations and generalizations regarding this role of laughter. Thomas Hobbes in the seventeenth century referred to laughter as a response to a feeling of "sudden glory." In the present century Sully, Sidis, Patrick, McDougall, Menon, and Rapp, among others, have examined laughter as a fundamental "means of rest and relaxation," "relief from restraint," "relief from great strain," a "release from a strained situation," a "release from inhibited emotions," a "means of avoiding psychic breakdown."

Two especially significant viewpoints are those of Bergson and Freud. Bergson's general contention (8–10) is that laughter functions as an agent in the adaptation of individuals as individuals and as members of collectivities to the ways and ideas and beliefs of the group or society. Men need to be constantly on the alert to discern the outlines of the current social situations, and to maintain a certain elasticity of mind and body to enable them to adapt themselves in consequence. Laughter points to the comic aspects of situations of rigidity and inelasticity, and corrects or at least relieves the rigidity. For Freud (229) laughter in general is the free discharge of psychic energy heretofore employed in areas in which this discharge has been inhibited. By means of the laughter "the static energy utilized in the inhibition has . . . suddenly become superfluous and neutralized. The laugher has laughed away the suppressed psychic energy." Montagu (1967: 78–84) recently has discussed laughter along with weeping and swearing as a "purgative" having "relief-purifying-pacifying effect," and thus enabling the individuals to re-establish their psycho-physical equilibrium.

We are more particularly concerned at this point with instances of laughter of the individual in concrete situations as he seeks remedial personal relaxation or release. The individual suffering a particularly painful and anxious experience often finds that a humorous attitude toward it and laughter about it takes the sting out of it by making it trivial or unreal or banal, or by depersonalizing it. Laughter at himself in a given situation, for example to cover his embarrassment at an off-color joke or upon having committed a social faux pas, assists him in recovering his composure and self-respect.

The significance of the individual's ability to laugh at himself is brought out in the following quotations. The first, from Armstrong (83), indicates what such laughter reveals about the laugher's social comprehension.

> The most salutary of all laughters, the laughter which is the greatest solvent of complications and the greatest civilizing force, is the laughter which we laugh at ourselves. For this laughter means always that we have laid bare and discarded some weakness, some power of injustice in ourselves, that we have risen to a higher understanding of others. A vain man, a frightened man, or an angry man cannot laugh at himself.

The second, from Gordon Allport (134), calls attention to the significance of laughter at self in the mental health of the individual and as a means of maintaining or restoring individual equilibrium—

> I venture to say that no person is in good health unless he can laugh at himself quietly and privately, noticing where he has overreached, where his pretensions have been overblown or pedantic. He needs to note when he has been hoodwinked, too sure of himself, too shortsighted, and above all, too conceited.

The laughter of the individual provides him other releases. His laughter in the enjoyment of the off-color or risqué situation may be his defense against forbidden fruit. Repressive laughter is for him a means of getting even with his oppressors and a mental out from under them. His aggressive laughter gets the aggressive drives and the hatreds and antipathies out of his system. Laughter is for him a means of living with annoyances, disappointments, failures, and frustrations; and of freely discharging repressed psychic energy and resentment, of restringing his bow, and of keeping on top of things. In some situations the laughter of the individual, like profanity, at least momentarily relieves him in a serious situation which threatens his well-being. It keeps him from blowing a fuse.

Friendly laughter helps him achieve personal social contentment and a feeling of peace and harmony with his social surroundings, and with mirthful laughter he gets the release and psychophysical exuberance that mirth gives.

Laughter serves other functions for the individual as actor among associates.

B. Laughter is a means of keeping up courage and of evading fear. We may laugh when we have narrowly escaped serious danger; for example, soldiers when a shell explodes killing others. "We may not only whistle but laugh to keep our courage up" (Flugel, 717).

C. Laughter can serve as an antidote to a feeling of inferiority. As the laugher laughs at his demeaning situations, at criticism, at insults, imagined or real, he provides himself with a sense of equality with, even superiority over, his detractors, and this helps him to maintain his self-confidence and self-respect. His feeling of weakness is compensated for by a feeling of strength (Rapp, 1951: 171; Myrdal, 960-961). By means of his laughter he sets himself aloof from the critics. Laughter becomes a sort of expression of triumph for him.

D. Laughter can serve as a device for avoiding or defending against social guilt. We, as individuals, may deflect, parry, turn away, or reduce the gravity of our guilt by laughing about it among others. If we can laugh wisely enough at ourselves and others (who also display our faults, weaknesses, inconsistencies, stupidities), the sense of dismay, guilt, anxiety, or fear can be lifted. To laugh at our blunders and errors, our faults and sins, is to some extent to surmount them.

E. Laughter may serve to deflect or cover up an insult or a mistake. A person does not want to acknowledge that he has been treated disrespectfully: he parries the thrust with a laugh. Similarly, he likes to divert attention from himself when he has pulled a boner in the presence of spectators: he may laugh the matter off, possibly resorting to a defiant I-can-take-it laugh. He saves face.

In connection with the last three propositions it can be noted that whether the individual laughs at himself privately or publicly involves different personal situations and different reactive effects. It may be generalized that when he laughs at himself privately he is either criticizing himself or in some measure reinstating himself in his own estimation. When he does so publicly, he is acknowledging fault, pleading pardon, or trying to relieve himself of embarrassment among his peers or the members of his reference groups. Laughter at himself may serve as a form of confession for himself, a doing of penance by himself, and the ensuing laughter of his fellows *at* and *with* him constitutes absolution by them.

F. Individuals who are living under conditions of horror and terror, subjugation and death—people in prisons, in concentration camps, soldiers at the front—by laughter at their situation are able to some extent to escape from the situation, to overcome their shock, to keep up their morale, even sanity, to rise above the situation.[1]

G. The individual may arouse laughter to protect himself. By telling an attention-shifting joke or a joke on someone else, the individual may with the ensuing laughter divert attention to some neutral subject or to someone else and away from his own faulty act. By telling a joke on someone else he may also be attempting to show that someone else's failure is at least as egregious as his own. The individual as a member of a discriminated against minority ethnic group may by jokes or stories about himself or his group invite laughter by the majority group to cover up a hapless situation.

H. Laughter can be undeniably a form of self-congratulation. The individual bursting with the feeling of having accomplished much, or having otherwise in his own opinion evidenced superiority or triumph over his kind, may at least salute himself with a laugh of commendation and exultation.

I. Feigned laughter is resorted to by the individual to render him several social services. He may simulate laughter to maintain personal standing among his associates. He may feel overlooked by his associates and indulge in conspicuous or boisterous laughter to attract attention to himself. Conversely, he may laugh in order not to be conspicuous. This may take several forms. He laughs in order to appear interested. The incident or joke or story may not seem funny to him, but he laughs out of deference to the speaker, or host, or boss. Perhaps he didn't get the point at all, but he joins heartily in the group laughter in order not to seem ignorant, stupid, or unsophisticated. He laughs to be "in." Mirth is sometimes shammed to cover up pain or some sensory defect, such as partial deafness. The ensuing laughter sidetracks attention until the individual can regain his poise.

---

[1] This is the laughter expressing "gallows humor," which will be discussed particularly with respect to its broader *social* therapeutic functions in chap. xii.

J. In extreme distress or despair, laughter may be for the individual a surrogate for weeping. Most persons suffer times of black discouragement or bitterness, of harrowing worry, or deep sorrow—tragic situations that invite weeping. But if they cannot weep or are afraid or ashamed to weep, they may laugh to hide their despair or sorrow or weakness. For them, as Hartly Coleridge put it,

> Laughter is oft but an art,
> To drown the outcry of the heart

Or a person in a strategic social position during time of tragedy and crisis may laugh to counteract the bleak state of mind and spirit of the people. Abraham Lincoln, during the darkest days of the Civil War, said, "I laugh because I must not cry. That is all. That is all."[2]

3. INDIVIDUAL DIFFERENTIALS AND RELATIVITIES

Nothing is funny or otherwise laughable to everybody all the time. What makes one person laugh makes another angry or bored; what makes one person laugh slips past another entirely because of inherent personal characteristics or because of inexperience with the particular type of situation. There is both individual and categorical differentiation in laughter-appeal and laughter-response among people. More explicitly, the laughter-provoking stimuli or messages are not received by all persons with uniformity of attention, perception, interest, understanding, or behavioral response.

The following are some of the main reputed or actually operative individual differentials.

A. Human beings as individuals differ greatly in their constitutional makeup. They differ in their physiological qualities, especially as these affect physical proficiency, vigor, and health.

---

[2] On what laughter does for the individual socius see also Freud, 138-142, 153-161, 177-218.

They differ in intelligence, in emotional and feeling potentials, in need-dispositions, in imagination, and in temperament. These greatly affect their behavioral probabilities. Each of these qualities also affects the degree to which the individuals are influenced by particular possible laughter situations. Ill health and anatomical defects and mishaps due to physical weakness just are not funny to the sick or infirm. In illness—for example, seasickness or airsickness—a funny story which normally would provoke laughter meets with no suitable response. What people laugh at when under the influence of alcohol or narcotics differs from what they laugh at when sober.

The more intelligent person sees laughable things and situations—oddities, incongruities, illogicalities, ludicrous occurrences or relations, the sharp point of a joke—that do not even catch the attention of the less mentally able. The moron often does not sense what those of normal mentality are laughing about—as we say, it goes over his head—and the imbecile does not laugh at all. The mentally less capable probably do more laughing with no objective cause—more giggling, more innocuous smiling. Intelligent members of an audience frequently will ignore trashy or stupid stuff that appeals to the mentally weak or deficient.

The hypergelast (the excessive laugher, the chronically garrulous person) will laugh at almost anything; many things that convulse him with merriment only evoke a smile, if that, in more normal folks. The agelast (the one who never laughs) and the misogelast(the anti-laugher or laughter-hater) are usually mentally or emotionally pathological and otherwise somewhat insensitive to the ways of their fellows.

Temperamental differences affect laughter behavior. Introverts seem to tend toward cognitive humor; their laughter results from the insightful integration of contradictory or incongruous ideas, attitudes, or sentiments which are experienced objectively. Extroverts tend more toward orectic humor, including humor with sexual or aggressive content (Berlyne, 809–810; Landis & Ross, 172). The stolid or impassive person perceives less and laughs less than the alert and sensitive one. Those of gay disposition laugh more than the soberly inclined. Those who are responsively sympathetic are more likely to be positive laughers than the hardhearted. The reserved and distant laugh less, individually and socially, than the hearty and cordial (Kambouropoulou, 38-40). Again, one person may greet a joke with a smile, another with body-shaking guffaws.

B.   Persons of different age levels react differently to possible laughter situations. Children have jokes which do not seem funny at all to grownups. Furthermore, as children grow older their sense of humor may change markedly; and there are marked variations from age period to age period in the kinds of situations which appeal to them as laughable. Much of what causes laughter among adults is of course quite out of the world of children. And situations which once inspired the aged to mirthful or satirical or aggressive laughter now have no effect on them.

C.   Evidence on the differences in what the sexes laugh at is inconclusive. Each sex, however, does have some peculiar areas of interest; for example, men are more given to laughing at situations connected with sports and economic and political conditions; women, at those connected with household matters and child raising. The sexes are not so likely to get the same point of the joke or satire regarding some situations, or are not involved enough to care. Of course, men laugh at the antics of women and vice versa. The sexes may also be trained differently as to what is laughable in some areas of life; for example, what it is permissible for a boy or girl to laugh at. (Rapp, 155–159; Coser, 1960: 84–85.)

D.   The differences between individuals seem in large measure to be due to conditioning and training. This in turn involves especially the amount, kind, and level of education received, the social class, the major life preoccupations, and the related perspectives of the individual. All of these produce in them different interests, values, habits, wishes, and the like.

Especially important, this training differentially affects their awareness of humor and their attitudes toward potential humorous situations. The cultural and social sophisticate sees humor in many more things and situations than the less sophisticated.

Thanks to the richness of his experience he can be mirthful about many more things and situations, real and imaginery, and about more subtle ones. The delicacy of a skillful pun is lost on the ignorant. Raucous horseplay humor offends the sensitive. A joke falls flat if addressed to a person not equipped to appreciate it.

Slapstick in drama or movies or TV programs seems to have a wide appeal among socially and culturally less sophisticated persons and among those of lower I.Q. Slapstick in amateur theatrics evokes uproarious laughter in the typical audiences.

Another readily observable example of special conditioning has already been indicated in our discussion of the laughter themes of groups (chap. v, sec. 2)—the differences in themes that prevail between individuals according to their highly determinative occupations or professions. Many of the jokes, caricatures, satirical comments, for instance, that priests, musicians, mail carriers, doctors, lawyers, soldiers, teachers, farmers, etcetera, exchange with each other with particular zest, satisfaction, and understanding involve conditions, things, and relations which are peculiar to their particular occupation or profession. Also, quite a number of the factors that produce laughter among them are unknown or less intelligible or unimportant to the members of other occupations.

The social standards that have become part of the individual's social status play an important part. For example, jokes involving contrasting sexual mores are very funny to those who have different standards; but are likely to be perplexing or insulting or grossly indecent to those who do not (Cameron, 93).

This resolves itself into what might be called the "interest stance" of the individual in the different types of situations. His special awarenesses and interests—the result of his social and cultural conditioning—lead or do not lead to automatic expectations with respect to the given situation. These, in turn, in considerable measure determine whether the juxtaposition of elements in the situation are laughable for him—whether his laughter is to be that of joy or amusement, of approval, disapproval, or hostility. The dog lover does not find jokes about dogs as nuisances or destroyers at all funny; in fact, they may enrage him.

In general, receptivity for and responsiveness to a given type of situation as a laughter situation varies not only with the differential characteristics of persons discussed immediately above, but also with others mentioned elsewhere in the present study, such as socioeconomic status, political persuasion, ethnic group and social class membership, and regional residence, for example, Texans and non-Texans (Koestler, 27–33).

4. THE PERSONALITY OF THE LAUGHER

Closely related to individual differentials in laughter is what can be told about individuals from their laughing behavior. The dry, mocking laugh, the nervous cackle, the sneering snicker, the booming guffaw, as well as the jovial or wholehearted and genuinely appreciative laugh, reveal attitudinal or emotional stance (Swabey, 2). What the individual most frequently and typically laughs at or about, and the tone of his laughter, tell much about his intellectual stature, his interests, his ethical principles and his morality, his social perceptions, his conceptions of decency, his personality traits in general. Certain kinds of jokes may particularly appeal to him, for example those involving sexuality or scatology, or those in some way expressing superiority or triumph over others. He will demonstrate characteristic personality tendencies. Murray in his study hypothesized that persons with strong self-assertive trends are likely to assume a critical, hostile and misanthropic attitude toward their fellow men, and found that those of his subjects with such traits intensely enjoyed disparagement jokes.

Whom the individual most frequently laughs with and against indicates the kind of crowd he runs with. The amount of laughing he does also indicates to some extent his good sense or lack of the same. The above mentioned hypergelast reveals lack of acumen, lack of control, and possibly lack of decency.

The laughter of an individual is thus to some extent both an indicator and an index of him as a person. Carlyle sensed this when he said, "How much lies in Laughter: the Cipher-key wherewith we decipher the whole man." Goethe also comprehended it: "Men show their character in nothing more clearly than by what they laugh at."

5.   THE INDIVIDUAL VICTIM OF LAUGHTER

The place of the various laughters of the individual in enabling himself as an individual to live comfortably and in more or less healthy social fashion among and with his associates was discussed earlier in the present chapter. But the individual may also be the victim, rightly or wrongly, of the critical, derisive, or hostile laughter of others. We are briefly concerned here with the effect of such laughter directed at him upon him. Almost every person dreads being laughed at.

Individuals, of course, differ in the degree to which they are affected when laughed at. Some have tougher hides than others; some can ignore the laughter of ridicule or censure or insult aimed at them. Or they can deliberately and willfully erect inner defenses against it. But most persons are shaken by it.

Usually, being laughed at causes more than just embarrassment. It may produce a variety of reactions in the victim depending upon his intellectual-temperamental makeup, his evaluation of those laughing at him, and his assessment of the strategic importance of the situation for himself. In general, though, the following are among the more typical potential effects.

A.   When the individual senses that people are laughing at him, it usually has a demeaning effect upon him; he feels humiliated, abashed, inferior. The implication is that he is weak, incompetent, not regarded as an equal.

B.   Some may suffer anxiety, or despair, or depression of spirit. The laughter of disapproval directed against the individual, whether justified or not, may produce in him a feeling of frustration, of failure, even defeat. He may successfully refute or deny the charges against him if made by language with precise statements presenting facts and logic, but he feels that his own puny counter-laughter is without effect as a neutralizing or counter-aggressive force.

C. It may develop a feeling of alienation from and/or of rejection by those laughing at the individual.

D. It may arouse anger at the laughers, or a spirit of rebellion against them or against their principles.

E. On the other hand, or in some situations combined with one or the other of the immediately preceding effects, being laughed at may cause the individual to check on himself. Why was he laughed at? What in his behavior brought on the criticism or censure? He may feel impelled to take stock of himself: "How am I doing? What is wrong with me?" Being laughed at may confront him with inconsistencies, incongruities, and ambiguities in his own behavior that he had been pushing back into his subconscious. The laughter may stir him out of his complacency into a more poignant self-consciousness and keener self-criticism. The very anticipation of being laughed at may have a chastening, precautionary, even corrective, effect; it may induce him to avoid stupidities, indecencies, bungling mishaps, and to do what he ought to do. Under some conditions the person laughed at and willing to concede the validity and justice of the implied charge may laugh at himself—an act which greatly contributes to his self-correction, as already noted.

F. The ability of the individual to stand up under laughter *at* him is usually evidence that he is behaviorally correct and secure in the given situation. You can joke with a person about a situation if his position or performance in it is secure and confident; but you cannot joke with him if there is grave doubt about either his sense of security or his self-confidence. The matter has been pointedly put: "If a man is happily married, you can say to him, 'Is your wife still living with you? How can she stand it?' But if a marriage is on or near the rocks, you can't joke about it." (Stylites, 239.)

G. Finally, the particular place of the individual in the particular social situation in which he finds himself also affects his laughter. This may be said to constitute an individual social-situation differential. His response may be the dignified smile or laugh of the hero who is being honored by the group he is in; or by contrast, it may be the embarrassed and perhaps forced laugh of one who has just made a fool of himself or suffered an indignity. Almost everyone laughs less boisterously when the joke is on himself.

Part Two

SOCIAL EFFECTS, FUNCTIONS AND USES OF LAUGHTER

VII.   Laughter as a Social Agent

Laughter is in considerable part a sociocultural product, as indicated previously. Equally significant, it is a widely available, potent, versatile, extensively and effectively utilized expressive and evocative means in interhuman affairs. It offers a variety of social and societal capabilities, functions, and utilities. Before taking up laughter as social agent, let us briefly examine a human capability which enables the individuals having it to play a dynamic part in many social situations.

1.   THE PERSON WITH A SENSE OF HUMOR AS SOCIAL AGENT

The person with a good sense of humor is often overlooked and unheralded as a key agent in human relations.[1] He can, and often does, carry on a number of strategic functions, whether in the affairs of the family or small groups, the crowd, the intragroup and intergroup activities of organizations, or in public life.

A.   The person with a sense of humor is able to play his important roles in social life because of certain rather typical characteristics and abilities. He is realistic; he sees persons and situations as they are; he is not confused or flimflammed. He gets behind the fictions, shams, and pretenses. He is in large measure able to free himself from his own subjectivities and uncertainties and objectively view other persons and social actions and conditions. Furthermore, he has a variety of attitudes and perspec-

---

[1] We are concerned here not with the mass-media humorist or comedian but with the person with more than an average sense of humor as he performs certain services for which he has special capability.

tives toward life, is not inflexible or bound down. He is imagina-
tive and cognitively creative. Also, a sense of proportion, as he
views the many angles and situations, governs his reaction to
them. By no means least, he can be playful about serious situations.

In simple language, the sense of humor is the ability to see
the funny side of things. But more specifically, and of focal importance in the present analytical context, it is the capacity of
the person to put two or more ideas, or practices, or conditions
in juxtaposition and detect and point out to himself and others
the unrealities, irrelevancies, illogicalities, or absurdities of the
persons and situations involved. His attitude toward the perpetrators of these, however, is usually not one of criticism or rancor
but of tolerance, even affection, toward his fellows, of understanding of them, and of amusement at their frailties. Also he
displays that essential and omnipresent element of humor in
general, the spirit of playfulness. These qualities he combines
with the relaxation of laughter. Of special significance, he has a
built-in check upon himself as he acts, namely, the supreme
quality of being able to laugh at himself.

B.   The person with a sense of humor can perform several
social functions that contribute to societal health and well-being.
First, with his well-directed jokes and other comic sallies and
pleasantries he can get in the open undercurrent conditions of
strain or danger in the group or particular relationship. Such
forewarning may forestall or prevent further deterioration of conditions, and even initiate or hasten corrective action.

Second, he may perform an adjustive function. By the laughter
induced among divergent, disparate, disorganized, disassociated
or hostile elements in a group, small or large, he relaxes, demo-
bilizes, reconverts, or rechannels the anger, or dissension, or feeling of distance that prevails among them. This produces an atmosphere of better temper, and tends to bring about a better
coordination or adjustment or equilibration of the incongruous or
discordant elements with each other.

Third, he may induce and manipulate laughter as an individual and social psychotherapeutic agent. Psychiatrists and social

psychologists have long recognized the value of this healing function. For the individual, a sense of humor is most helpful in maintaining and improving his own mental health. It enables him to see and assess his own condition in a realistic, but humorous, light. The very laughter at himself highlights some of the unrealities and contradictions in his mental stance with respect to himself and the world, and invites a saner attitude. As a dynamic factor in a group or other social psychic relationship, by his humorous tactics in getting the people involved to laugh at themselves and with each other, he can reduce or dispel the individual and/or social-psychic tension, strain, worry, or fear that distracts them. The laughter blunts or softens the sharp thrust of the incidents that produce the strain or pain, and drains off the psychopathic pressures. In general, the man with a sense of humor, especially if he combines it with social initiative, can get people back on the track—back into attitudes and behaviors which are essential to intelligent, peaceful, effective, and wholesome social interaction. Finally, due to his creative ability he frequently is able to modify beneficially, or even invent new, superior ways and means dealing with social situations.[2]

2. LAUGHTER AS SOCIAL INSTRUMENT

Laughter is a potent instrument in influencing human actions, feelings, thoughts, and decisions. Its different functional types are involved in different kinds of situations in which different kinds of social activities are conducted, and have their societal and cultural effects, sometimes seemingly quite inconsistent with each other. As engaged in, individually or collectively; unconsciously, incidentally or spontaneously; or consciously, deliberately and purposively (depending on the type of situation and the relations of the actors), it is an agent in the conduct of a large number of social, sociopsychological, and societal functions. Some of these functions are quite incidental and unplanned, and

---

[2] On the sense of humor and its social utility see Mikes, 13-14; Rapp, 1951: 163-171; Kimmins, 439; Goodchilds & Smith; Onwake.

are sometimes unanticipated as to effects. But the significant fact is that laughter is widely resorted to as a social utility to accomplish social purposes and ends.

What is more, it is an agent of subtle potency. It can produce social effects when argument and logic and even force have proved themselves ineffective; for in laughter we tap something much deeper and more elemental than logic, and often more persuasive than force.

The effectiveness of laughter as a social influence and a social instrument in the career of human beings is brought out by the fact that very young children—before they are able to talk, or perhaps even before they get much effect from articulate speech of others—are attuned to it as a highly influential factor in their behavior. Very small children have joy in joint laughter. It is astonishing how early in their life children become highly sensitive to laughter as a set of social signals expressing the affection, approval, disapproval, and criticism of others. With them it is often more effective than words. Children parry disapproving words of others, especially their peers, with words of their own, but many are helpless when exposed to the highly derisive or abusive laughter of the peers, and often will flee from the scene. It is astonishing how early children learn to solicit approving laughter.

The different social effects, functions and/or uses of laughter[3] involve different kinds of laughter depending on the interactional position of the respective laughers. The different kinds of laughter have a variety of possible social functions and uses. In the case of laughter as a unifier, or group-maintaining or tension-releasing agent, it is in most instances laughing *with* or laughing *together*. As a social control or social corrective activity, it consists in laughing *at* the violators and deviants. In laughter which separates, isolates, or excludes a portion of those in interaction, the intended or actual victims are laughed at by insiders, who are trying to exclude them. Laughter as a weapon or as a conflict

---

[3] The social effects, functions, and uses cannot be entirely separated. What occurs in a particular situation has an effect which may be of marked functional significance and which may be consciously induced because of its potential utility.

or aggression technique is directed *at* or *against* the opponents.

The range of societal effects, functions, and uses of laughter is great, extending from its effectiveness as a unifying-binding and as an equalizing agent at one extreme to its effects as a separative, excluding, and conflict device at the other. The different sociological conceptualizations of effects-functions-uses will be examined along a continuum with the above mentioned extremes at the respective poles, and with laughter as involved in group maintenance, social control, assimilation, social conservation, social renovation and reorganization, the status system, and its therapeutic functions in the easing of social tensions and adjustment to adversities in between.[4]

An outstanding but generally overlooked benefit of laughter as a functional agent in societal operation is that it is an economical aid—almost a gift—in getting things done. Laughing with and at people is a universal and ubiquitous human trait. Such laughter appears spontaneously in many types of social situations, and in its basic forms need not be developed through social conditioning procedures nor stimulated for the particular situation. It is, in fact, set off almost automatically in many typical interactions. Moreover, it operates *directly* among participants and upon targets. On the other hand, the arbitrary and purposive application of physical, psychological, and social force in societal operation is arduous and requires great expenditure of society's energy. In the main, force must be institutionalized, and increasingly instrumented organizationally. But in many situations laughter is self-starting, and works without specific inducing or societal machinery, yet has a powerful bearing on those involved. As an often unobtrusive substitute it makes some of this formalized functioning unnecessary; and it can function as an economical supplementary operational aid.

This feature of laughter is evident in the general maintenance of social systems as it draws people together, as it does its work

---

[4] It should be clear that when we discuss laughter as a factor in various social functionings in the ensuing chapters we do not mean to imply that it is the sole factor. There are, for example, other ways of expressing social solidarity, or social superiority, or social antipathy besides laughter.

of instructing, warning, correcting, coercing, compelling, punishing, as it eases divergence of interests and releases tensions and frustrations, as it enables the contestants in conflict situations to safely bypass the physical showdown. A good laugh may contribute more than vocal or written admonitions or commands; it may be easier, cheaper, and more successful than laws and ordinances, police and supervisors, hierarchical chain of command, or other regulative and operative personnel and organizational machinery.[5]

3. HUMOR AND LAUGHTER IN ROLE PERFORMANCE

Much of our social activity consists in performing our various roles in our groups and our society. Role confusion and inconsistency are widespread factors in the provoking of mirth, and humor and laughter are omnipresent factors in the maintenance of roles and in accurate, adequate, and consistent performance.

Social roles are the socioculturally defined, patterned, and standardized ways of behavior expected of actors by virtue of their social positions in all of the typical relationship situations of a given social system. For the individual the role is the specific configuration of standard performance obligations, taboos, and permissives that attach to each type of social situation in which he participates. Needless to say, he performs many and varied roles, voluntarily or involuntarily, with varying degrees of success.

It is often not realized that considerable laughter, whether of individuals or collectivities, occurs when role performance upsets expectations. We laugh when persons in some way depart from the standard behavior set for them as friends, parents, children, husbands and wives, followers of vocations, members of particular types of social groups, members of social classes or ethnic or nationality groups, occupants of other hierarchical strata, or in almost any other activity characteristic of or essential to a social system. The lapse or irregularity of role performance may be that noted in the actual observed behavior of per-

---

[5] On this economical aspect of laughter see Rapp, 1947: 207-219, and 1951: 41.

sons or groups or as presented in a joke, cartoon, comedy, comic strip, caricature, or satirical piece. The laughter-arousing situations may be those of role confusion, role inconsistency, role contradiction, role misunderstanding, role uncertainty, role ignorance, role inadequacy, role ineptness or some other ambiguity in role performance. More concretely, the humorous misfiring may be that of neophyte role performers: immigrants, strangers, newlyweds; of persons with some subnormal physico-psychic condition: a fuddy-duddy forgetting or confusing the essential rules, the absent-minded oldster, the inebriate; those overplaying an aspired-to role: the child trying to act like an adult, the mature matron acting like a simpering teen-ager, the *nouveau riche* climbers mis-acting in the rarefied upper stratum. But whatever the situation the lapse in role performance is a copious source of mirth.

The humor and laughter relating to role performance renders two important social services. First, the individual role performer by means of laughter at himself is often able to face and resolve his own role uncertainties, inconsistencies and mishaps, and save himself possible personality damage, and thus not impair the operation of his group.

Second, there is a societal gain. The role system is the means by which a group or society gets its necessary action from its members in the right way and at the right time on every particular situation. The laughter at role confusion, inconsistency, or ineptness makes for an articulation and underscoring of essential requirements in role performance, points to inadequacy of social action in meeting these requirements, and suggests correction or improvement. It is thus important in maintaining the role system, and contributes to group or societal support.

4. THE PROFESSIONAL AND ORGANIZATIONAL PRODUCTION OF LAUGHTER

Humor is supposed to spring up spontaneously in certain kinds of social interaction, with laughter making its almost automatic correlative appearance. Note, however, that not only have humorous situations and circumstances been studiously contrived, and laughter deliberately evoked for a variety of purposes, but this has been done by specialist funnymen and funmakers.

"Fools" are perennial figures in social life. They have appeared in many forms and under many names: plain fool, zany, rustic, boor, simpleton, clown, jester, buffoon, and others. They have long been closely associated with laughter. In general, the laughter is occasioned by the amusement the fools afford their observers or audiences with their apparent or pretended exaggerations, deficiencies, errors, irresponsibilities, absurdities, stupidities, or other deviations from the normal, and, thus, their rejection of standard values and their freedom from the bonds of society's proprieties, conventions, mores, and other normalcies.

The laughter, whether at or with or because of the fool, has varied with the kind or type of fool. It is especially significant that some of this laughter has been incidental and spontaneous and some specifically sought for, designed and elicited. Importantly, at different times in history societies have had a category of fools sometimes referred to as institutionalized fools who have not contributed to laughter-provoking entertainment merely incidentally but have been assigned or granted the occupational role of deliberately providing it. These have been more than tolerated: they have been given a sort of licensed freedom. Furthermore, they have often enjoyed a distinctive and even high status in their societies. The range and variation of these career fools has been great.

The least "professional" of the institutionalized fools have been those funny in their particular societies because of their physical deformities or other grotesque physical characteristics (e.g., dwarfs, hunchbacks, some cripples, some overly obese persons), or psychic deficiencies or aberrations (feeble-mindedness, dementia, or other psychopathic condition). In imperial Rome wealthy householders had such fools, and deformed and imbecile creatures fetched high prices in the slave market. References to such fools reappear in Europe in the twelfth century and increase in the fourteenth and fifteenth centuries, particularly in French account books. Almost all known peoples have at one time or another utilized such fools as entertainers.

Alongside these pitiful creatures there have been the artificial, or mock, or professional fools—the *actors* for whom performance as a fool was a special occupational role and consciously pursued as such. They learned and performed their routines as professional comedians. Fools of this kind have included the jesters, clowns, buffoons, and other comic actors.

Fools of one kind or another were attached to the courts (e.g., privileged royal jesters), to the private households of the wealthy, to corporations, to taverns, even to brothels. Some were fools in the comedies of the theaters; some were clowns, tricksters, and jokesters at carnivals and fairs. The roles of the merry-andrews of Elizabethan England, the Pierrots of Old France, the Harlequins of medieval Italy and later of English comedy we know of today. In some periods, for example the Renaissance, some of these were famous. To be a jester or buffoon of a special type for a king or lord or wealthy family, or to be a member of a well-known troupe of public entertainers was a walk of life not to be despised either by a man or by his friends; and the jokes or other witty sallies that he made were "negotiable securities of first-hand values," as Hazlitt put it.

It is of special point that the fools were types of persons who were maintained in the society for the express purpose of making people laugh. The poor simpleton, dwarf, or cripple was selected for the role because the society considered his grotesque body or his pathetic antics to be funny. The business of the professional comedian, trained for his established and standardized role, was to contrive situations and engage in actions that made laugh-making provide a livelihood, and some of them made a great deal of money.[6]

Today we have our kinds of privileged jesters and clowns. Laughmaking by them is an enterprise of no mean proportions, both in terms of the number, prominence, and prestige of the professional personnel, and of financial outlay such as production costs and the remuneration of the performers. A conspicuous

---

[6] On the social functions performed by other categories of fools see Klapp, 1949; Daniels & Daniels; Berlyne, 812; and especially Klapp, 1962.

body of performers are those connected with "big-time show biz." This includes the performers in the television and radio comedy shows (Bob Hope, Jackie Gleason, Jack Benny, Ed Sullivan, Dean Martin, Johnny Carson, and so on), some of whom have an international reception; the hundreds of professional jokesters who do the night-club circuits and the summer and winter resorts; and the actors in the motion-picture and stage comedies.

The creators of syndicated cartoons and comic strips get through to vast numbers of people. Less widely read but significant are the creators of the syndicated columns and the volumes of jokes, and the rather small, select body of humorous essayists and of writers of humorous short stories and verse and jocular satirical columns.

These professionals, especially those in show business, commonly enjoy high popularity and renown. An impressive number receive fabulous incomes. Some of the most prominent are multimillionaires. Someone has remarked, "Comedian Bob Hope has made millions out of laughing matters."

In the United States we have a laughter-producing industry that operates according to modern big-business methods. Many of the laughter-evoking materials are produced by crews, or teams, of specialists in what might be referred to as shops or factories. These consist of researchers for and creators and other processors of, and of buyers and traders in humorous materials. Out of the materials thus acquired the industry makes its readily assimilable and saleable jokes, cartoons, comic strips, comic books, movie and television comedies, and so on. There is a legitimate commerce in jokes and gags manufactured by the factories just mentioned, and these are sold to the performers and organizations in the radio and TV industry. But there is also a bootleg trade in stolen jokes and gags. This commerce involves huge sums of money, since a good gag has a high price.

Much of this product is standardized as to form and theme and is in effect as well packaged for the consumer as cigarettes or aspirin or breakfast food. Furthermore, the vast proportion of the materials produced are syndicated—systematically distributed over the nation by mass-supermarketing facilities such as radio and TV chains, newspapers, and firms publishing comic books.

In the modern world with its vast mass-communication resources the professional humorists have unprecedented opportunity to provide the people with humor and laughter.

The people, historically and contemporaneously, have constituted a vast patronage for what the generators of laughter produce. The people cannot be happy, efficient, and sane without the great variety of individual and social boons provided. They seek laughter, and each society has had its particular types of suppliers to meet the demand. In our society the specialists meet the demands of audiences ranging from near illiterates to ultra-sophisticates. Of special point, many of the consumers, chary of supporting some other social agents, have been willing to pay a good price for their laughter.

VIII. Group and Societal Maintenance

Laughter is an important factor in expressing and indicating group and societal unity and solidarity, and in inducing and maintaining all manner of collectivities from simple primary groups to a complex society. Some of the more outstanding theoretical features of laughter in the formation, organization, and operation of group structures will be examined.

1. JOINED LAUGHTER AND GROUP AWARENESS

When a number of people laugh together, they have a basis for at least a temporary grouping. They are psychically interacting with each other and are receiving communications from each other; they are bound together by the common interest in the laughter theme; and as they laugh together there is a heightening of awareness, both to themselves and to the outsiders, of their collective identity, and thus of their existence as a group.

2. THE ASSOCIATIVE EFFECT OF JOINED LAUGHTER

Joined laughter, whether that of shared mirth, joy, triumph, scorn, or protection has a unifying, annealing, consolidating effect upon those laughing *with* each other. When we laugh together (*a*) we create easy, open communication among us; (*b*) we are as individuals somewhat liberated from our individual eccentricities and rigidities of feeling, emotion and thinking, and enjoy a common state of euphoria; (*c*) for the time being at least, we push aside, or submerge, or even cancel conceptions of insufficiencies, diversities, even failures of our associates; (d) we recognize and accept one another as fellow human beings, as comrades sharing a significant common experience; (e) we ignore or unconsciously overlook the differences and possible sources of dissension among us, and interact as brothers or friends; we may, in fact, be evidencing the spirit of reconciliation; (f) we are sharers of at least a momentary common lot, which produces a sense of accord, a state of rapport, and consensus for the time being, and we express our "empathic participation with others;" (g) we close ranks, and function as a united, integrated, cohesive body. (Duncan, 1953: 49–50; 1962: 330; Wolff, Smith, & Murray, 346.)

3. LAUGHTER AS INDICATOR OF TOGETHERNESS

Within a given group joined laughter indicates that a fair degree of unity, solidarity, freedom from friction and antagonism, and reciprocity prevails. Group leaders and societal governors over the millennia have been aware, as an ancient proverb puts it, that a happy social condition exists when "all the people are laughing together."

Laughing together freely and jovially is a pleasant experience for the people. Usually it means that reciprocally humane attitudes prevail, that they not only tolerate and accept each other, but that social amity exists among them, and that they are in a state of physical and sociopsychological health and well-being.

4. INDUCED JOINED LAUGHTER AS UNIFIER

Joined laughter also is deliberately brought about to effect unification. By opening with a laugh, the public speaker quickly and easily unites his audience, and wins them to his side for the moment at least. The host or hostess attempts to induce joined laughter as a means of "building up" a dinner party that is not going too well. Everyone is aware of the unifying effect of a number of people laughing together while viewing a TV comedy.

Developing common laughter in a group torn by friction, dissension, antagonism or separatism is an open and simple way of re-establishing communication. More, it tends to soften or neutralize existing animosity and discord, helps to cool indignation and dispel divisive prejudices. It not only maintains but also reaffirms and substantiates the group's bonds for the members, at least for a time.

Especially significant also is the unifying and solidifying effect on a group (or class or other collectivity) of being ridiculed, lampooned, and laughed at by outsiders. Critical or antagonistic laughter pulls the group together and causes it to cling more firmly to its principles and objectives.

5. THE EXPRESSION AND MAINTENANCE OF GROUP VALUES AND STANDARDS

Laughter within a group is a means of expressing and maintaining the group values and standards. For example, laughter directed at the parvenu, the eccentric, the cheap climber, the troublemaker, the fool, etcetera, is a means of indicating defection from the standards of the group, as well as of underscoring principles of action. It also reaffirms for the laughers the support of the standards, and thus aids in maintaining the ascendancy of the group for its members vis-à-vis other groups. Similarly, the laughter emanating from the group members is a method of attacking all insincere or seemingly harmful individual or factional claims, pretentions, and novelties within the group.

6. INTERPERSON COMPATIBILITY

Participation in the common group laughter is an evidence of the compatibility of the individual members with the group. Those who refuse to join in it are frowned upon as bad sports or dissenters. Conversely, when a person invites laughter from his group and the invitation is not accepted, he feels out of place (Coser, 1959: 172); as we say, he falls flat on his face. Furthermore, the laughter of associates, whether open or restrained, indicates whether the individual is behaving acceptably or otherwise in the group or organization. This is of special significance for new members.

7. MORALE AND ESPRIT DE CORPS

Closely related is the fact that laughter within the group about some mutually satisfying situation among the members, or laughter directed against disturbing outsiders, is an important factor in enhancing the morale of the members of the ingroup and in protecting it against disruptive influences from without (Rinder). As between groups, when "we" laugh together, it strengthens the boundaries between us and "them" who do not know what we are laughing at, or who are not laughing with us. Furthermore, laughter *at* foreign groups usually helps to build the esprit de corps of the given group.

8. REFLECTOR OF GROUP DISLIKE AND DISUNITY

The laughter of groups, however, may also indicate the opposite conditions and affect of the above. If it is free and happy joined laughter, it seems to be a unifier and evidence of unity, solidarity, compatibility and morale as indicated. But if it is not, it may reflect aloofness of the members of each other or dislike and disunity among them. This is brought out by the joking in a group. People who like one another feel free to joke good-naturedly with or kid one another. If there is indifference or actual disliking, there usually is little or no joking. If the situation is one of disliking, ". . . the joking is likely to be vicious, disparaging, and biting," For example, "The nature of the joking among the children in a classroom, among members of a team, or among members of a school staff may reveal much about the strength of the effect linkages of the group." (Torrance.)

9. EASING INTERNAL DIVERGENCE OF INTERESTS AND HOSTILITY

The display of humor and the accompanying laughter play an important part in the easing and expediting of relationships between members of groups and between persons and parties in organizations (Blau, 91–95) or in communities where there is some divergence of interests and hence the possibility of disagreement, tension, hostility, separation, and conflict: as for example, among competitors of similar jobs in a commercial or industrial establishment, members of different status levels in an organizational hierarchy, as well as among members of different social classes (cf. chap. xi) and ethnic groups in the community. In many such situations disjunction can be avoided and conjunction maintained by joking, and friendly teasing, and jovial manners, and the accompanying euphoria of laughter (Bradney). Similarly, laughing together within a group that has suffered internal opposition may function as a means of reconciliation. Group-wise, community-wise, society-wise, "humor is one of the ways in which human beings can attain a meager sense of their own brotherhood" (Rovit, 244), and laughing together is "a way of keeping social bridges in good repair" (Duncan, 1962: 259).

10. A SPUR TO ACTION

Laughter is also a spur to action in behalf of the group or society. In general, it is a sharp and telling instrument utilized by the rank and file members to prod the slow, the listless, the failing among them. The special public funmakers—the professional jokesters, cartoonists, satirists—are also always on the trail of the group leaders, the public functionaries, those otherwise socially conspicuous, to energize them, and demand prompt, efficient, and intelligent service.

11. LAUGHTER TACTICS BY GROUPS TO PROTECT THEMSELVES

Laughter is employed by the group, as by the individual (chap. vi, sec. 2C, D, E), to protect itself against criticisms made of it or possible affronts directed against it.

The joined laughter of the members against criticism from without unites and unifies them, as we have indicated. But it also gives them a feeling of strength in resisting the critical or derisive assault of outside individual or group attackers. It is a sort of shield which protects them as it deflects or repels the antipathetic barbs of the assailants.

An equally significant historical use of laughter by groups or collectivities, as well as by individuals (chap. vi, sec. 2G) has been that of inviting laughter at themselves as a means of coping with possible critics, or with non-friendly or prejudiced attitudes toward them. This includes its use as a means of ingratiating themselves with the potential or actual unfriendly population elements, and thus halting or deflecting demeaning or antagonistic action.

Freud (166) long ago called attention to the tactics of some Jews in directing humor and wit at themselves, especially in the form of jokes about their own peculiarities invented by themselves and told to non-Jews. This use of laughter has been intended to ease communication and relieve embarrassment between Jew and non-Jew, and especially to resolve or deflect hostile interest or intent away from the Jew, and thus to forestall possible indecency or antipathy on the part of the non-Jew.[1]

Such use of laughter at selves has been employed by members of other minority groups to protect themselves against the majority members. Some Negro slaves, and contemporary "Uncle Toms," have appeased the white man by ridiculing their own behavior, including their deviations from the white majority's values and codes.

One observer of the American scene (Myrdal, 960) has stated: "The loud high-pitched cackle that is commonly considered as the 'negro laugh' was evolved in slavery times as a means of appeasing the master by debasing oneself before him and making him think that one was contented." This use of laughter by groups under the type of situation indicated can be thought of as a survival tactic.

12.   LAUGHTER IN SOCIOCULTURAL ASSIMILATION

A final aspect of laughter as it functions in a community or society is the part it plays in sociocultural assimilation, especially that of immigrants and ethnic minorities.

A.   Sociocultural assimilation is the process whereby the

---

[1] On jokes by Jews about themselves see Stephenson; Rosenberg & Shapiro.

various social and/or cultural segments of a community or society come to be merged, coalesced, absorbed, and incorporated into a relatively solidary and cooperative society that is unified and homogeneous in essential attitudes, ideas, values, objectives, loyalties and major social activities. Mainly, it involves changes in these essential features of social life on the part of the minority group members with their divergent features. In the process the newcomers, recent "outsiders" or "aliens," existent ethnic minorities, on the one hand, slough off many of their native sociocultural features, especially those sharply differing from and incompatible with the over-all society and its culture, and abandon old-country or other minority-group ways, ideals, loyalties, and allegiances. On the other hand, they take on the ways of the larger society, develop a feeling of loyalty to it, and participate in it with normal efficiency and success. When the process has run its typical course, they no longer think or act differently from the existing group, and consequently no longer are viewed as outsiders by the larger body. They have become full-fledged members of the group or society.

B. The laughter of the larger group is a spontaneous assimilative pressure that the unassimilated have difficulty in escaping from. The key aspect of the situation, of course, is the desire on the part of the newcomers or other ethnic elements *not* to be laughed at, condescendingly or sardonically, as people who are *conspicuously* different. The effect of this critical laughter may be more penetrating, more lingering, and more poignantly felt than the influence or pressure exerted by the sterner organized agencies specifically charged with such functions.

In our own American history the successive waves of immigrant greenhorns wherever they settled, and the country jakes, hillbillies, and southern Negroes coming to strange regional or city environments, have been subjected to critical laughter because of their foreign "uncouth" habits, clothes, speech forms, and other ways. As soon as these became conscious of the derisive or derogatory communicative content of laughter at them by the representatives of the larger whole, it did several things: first, it revealed to them the standards of behavior and belief that they would have to conform to in order to avoid being laughed at; and second, it operated as a powerful force in motivating them to take on the majority ways.

C. It has already been indicated (sec. 3 above) that joined laughter *within* a group or community or society is both a means and an indication of unification and cohesion. Related to this, group laughter also serves both as test and as index of assimilation into the group or society.

When the members of heretofore socioculturally different and differentiated groups—the minority groups—can laugh together knowingly and meaningfully with the majority it means that they have acquired very many of the common values, interests, and beliefs, and habits, mores, and institutional ways of the general population. When they have reached this state, they are usually accepted as full-fledged fellow members by the majority. They can then be said to have reached a high degree of assimilation. The growth, increasing spontaneity, and prevalence of such joined laughter similarly can be viewed as a sort of index of the *progress* of assimilation of the population elements.

The intergroupal laughter is evidence not only that a considerable degree of cultural uniformity has occurred but also that the majority elements have little or no consciousness of difference, little or no feeling of superiority, and exercise little or no discrimination; nor do the minority elements feel inferior and excluded. The common laughter implies a common consciousness and a sense of community.

A final decisive reflector of assimilation is that in our present pluralistic society our people of Polish, Italian, German, Scandinavian, Greek, Irish, East European and other national descent can safely, good-naturedly, even joyfully, josh with or about one another and laugh at one another—which indicates tolerance based on mutual acceptability.

IX. Laughter and Social Control

One of the strategic aspects of group or societal maintenance is social control.

Every society must have social order; that is, conformity to its basic norms, harmonious and coordinated interaction of its people, adequate performance of their various roles by the people in the conduct of the society's essential social functions, continuous socially constructive action, and *pari passu*, avoidance of societal inefficiency, waste, vice, friction, conflict, or other disorderly action. Social control refers to that congeries of mechanisms and processes by which the group resists harmful variations from itself and ensures that social order and effective operation is maintained. Factors which produce high social temperature must be regulated, reduced, rectified, or eliminated. Where there is low social temperature there must be boosting and restoration. Always there must be inculcation, critical examination, discipline, correction. In every community or society much informal pressure is also exerted on individuals, groups and other collectivities which has a socially controlling, though not necessarily beneficial, effect.

1. LAUGHTER AS AN AGENT OF SOCIAL CONTROL

Laughter as exercised by the group, community, or society is an act of passing judgment on social performance, and functions as a sort of governor in human affairs. It serves several closely related social-control functions.

A. Some of what the social entity laughs at, and most of what it laughs against, as implied in another connection in section 5 of the preceding chapter, indicates what is not acceptable to it, what is not in conformity with its principles and standards of social order and well-being. This is, in effect, a form of instruction—the exercise of a didactic function. What constitutes objectionable social deviation is underscored and dramatized, and positive social behavioral requirements (the social rules), the goals of action, and the criteria of correctness and propriety are highlighted by contrast and are promulgated.

The critical social laughter provides special leads that individuals should heed regarding the types of persons laughed at. Among the more frequently expressed categories are (1) incompetents, especially ludicrous role failures such as naive newcomers, *nouveaux riches*, hicks, dupes, easy marks, fools, frauds; (2) people who profess to be more than they are: pretenders, imposters, humbugs, windbags, stuffed shirts, pompous asses, showoffs, upstarts, including the falsely humble, as well as the vain; (3) certain non-conforming types: some fanatics, some deviants, some outsiders, oddballs, and beatniks; (4) certain overconformers, such as yes-men, mock heroes, and some of the over-ritualized.[1]

B.   Most people are sensitive to the antagonistic laughter of other people of their groups, or community, or society. The various types or categories whose laughter they fear are varying with each relational or functional situation: the majority on a particular issue, key people with respect to a particular situation, the peer groups to which the individuals belong, the reference groups by which they judge themselves, the people or groups highly regarded for one reason or another by the potential targets, socially powerful people such as the community power elite or the authorities of the important social institutions, higher-ups in the hierarchical systems (organizational, social class [status], absolutistic rulers in totalitarian political economic setups, local social arbiters). The laughter of such societal segments is felt as a potent influence. The potential or actual targets are aware that the influential by their approving laughter can

---

[1] On types of persons in American society against whom critical or sardonic laughter is directed see Klapp, 1962: 73-80.

make them socially as individuals or families or other groups and by their hostile laughter can break them. The laughter of people thus creates a pressure to conform to social objectives and demands and to avoid what is criticized.

Most men also feel that they must abide by the pressures emanating from the mass. This often means going along with the herd, as mentioned in Chapter II, in order to avoid its ridicule, condemnation, exclusion, or the necessity of self-defense. This herd pressure can kill personal eccentricity and social deviation, but it can also smother innovation and variation. The infectiousness and herd power of laughter means also that by manipulating it, many people can be moved to respond en masse and thus direct their approval or amusement, or ire, or fear, or ridicule at what or who is to be laughed *at*. In some types of social situations the laughter of the collectivity functions as a form of persuasion, even as a form of compulsion.

C. Some socially induced laughter is purposive and intended to operate as a form of censure. Whether the laughter emerges from the rank and file or from professional jokesmiths and satirists, it functions as an efficient instrument for expressing criticism and disapproval. By means of their laughter the observers poke fun at our individual and group follies and foibles and futilities. The stern fact, though, is that the laughter is a way of blaming and condemning us for our foolishness, ignorance, silliness, stupidity, or absurdity; for our weak-mindedness or absent-mindedness; for our mendacity, indency, or uncouthness; for our extravagance; for our departure from decorum or justice; for our logical incoherence or incongruity. By no means least, the laughter of contempt can point to and condemn serious anti-social behavior in every institutionalized area of social life. It points accusingly and censoriously at our social and societal failure.

D. The person or group not only suffers censure by being laughed at but may also endure humiliation, be punished by, and even suffer exclusion from the company of associates. No punishment, for example, is more real or severe for all but the most thick-skinned or stupid than to be made the laughing stock of the group or community. Such effects may be the specific intention of the participant laughers. The laughter thus may prove to be a kind of intimidation, castigation, or punishment.

E. It is obvious that laughter as a means of instruction, censure, and punishment becomes both socially disciplinary and socially corrective, with decided admonitive, directive, and preventive capability. As Bergson (17) so cogently summarizes, "It 'makes us . . . endeavor to appear what we ought to be."[2] It reminds us of our place and proper action in our group and in our interaction with others in our community; it most sharply indicates our errors of behavior that need correction; and its continual threat as a means of public warning, humiliation, ridicule, and possibly excommunication or even more drastic punishment keeps us alert to social prohibitions and requirements "By laughter society avenges itself for the liberties taken with it" (Bergson, 197).

F. A further social control aspect of laughter is its efficacy as a debunking and unmasking agent that protects the group or the community against being misinformed and misled. Joined laughter of the collectivity has often been a quite spontaneous means of showing up or deflating the frequently derided social types indicated above and of penetrating and destroying social shams. But it has also been fomented for such purposes by leaders and factions.

Laughter is a potent way of exposing our self-deceptions, dogmatisms, and pedantries, our exaggerations, and our gross misapprehensions of what is going on. It is a corrector of the affectation and self-importance of beggars and kings. In general it can unmask both our lapses and excesses.

G. Laughter is not slowed by any need to interpret laws, nor is it debated and argued in the courts, nor does it require the operation of ponderous law-enforcing and penal organizations. Usually it operates spontaneously, quickly, and summarily as a social policeman.

H. Thus far we have discussed the laughter that exercises

---

[2] On laughter as a corrective see also Grieg, 189-191.

negative social control: the laughter that disapproves, restrains, or prohibits incompetent, stupid, pretentious and anti-social behavior, and hence functions as a stern corrective. But we must not overlook the part of positive laughter (cf. chap. iv, sec. 5) in stimulating, promoting and maintaining positive social control. The positive controls involve processes which deliberately persuade, induce, stimulate, direct, excite, and motivate to acceptable, desirable, and essential conduct. These give the persons and groups controlled satisfying outlets for their energies, invite positive action and social expression, and lead to the establishment, cultivation, and enhancement of orderliness, cooperation, social production, harmonization, self-control, respect for others, and general goodwill.

The positive laughters—the invitational and inspirational laughter or smile, the laughter or smile of recognition and encouragement, of approval and applause, of sympathy and empathy—are potent in positive control. Friends, parents, teachers, administrators, leaders of men have long since learned the value of such laughters in effecting behavior contributory to and consonant with positive social objectives and ends. Such laughters are regulative, but they add new dimensions to social action as they sustain, enthuse, stimulate, and inspire people; motivate them to *want* to act in a constructive, even creative, social way in their respective societal niches and roles; and reward them with sought-after, overtly distinguishable signs of approbation.[3]

2. SATIRE AND ITS LAUGHTER IN SOCIAL CONTROL

Satire is a humorous critical response to the behavior of human beings as individuals, to types of persons, to the actions of human collectivities (groups, organizations, social classes, nations), to ideological and social movements, to social conventions and institutions. It is the end result of indignation due to awareness of existential abuses, errors, indecencies, dishonesties,

---

[3] For a special analysis of laughter as a social sanction see Piddington, 115-123.

stupidities, superfluities, perversions, injustices of mankind, or other departures from common sense or the established norms and ways. It always has an aim, a preconceived purpose, with respect to these situations. This is, first, to pinpoint, and then to ridicule, usually also to censure, and in its extreme usage to punish, the individual or collective violators of the norms. Second, and not infrequently, it is to bring about improvement, to encourage or inaugurate reform.

Satire exercises its critical appeals through its comic perceptions. Humor is an essential and identifying element. The comic perceptions are aroused in the audience by appeals to common sense and reason as the treatment depicts the incongruities of the situation: the gap between the criticized existential and the reasonable, essential, or correct. The humor of satire may be amiable, almost playful and good-temperedly jocular; but it may also be sardonic, biting, or caustic and furiously denunciatory.

The satirist, a sort of judge who also shows some of the attitude of the prosecutor, aims at exposing and denouncing the follies and faults of the individuals, collectivities, and institutions in question, and often of pronouncing sentence upon them.

An almost invariable accompaniment of the humor and of the main enforcing aids of the satirical effort is the laughter which ensues from the effective performance of the satirist. It may range from the smile of amusement or amazement to a quite obviously angry psychophysical rumble. It is an expression of irritation, disgust, outrage, contempt, even hatred. It invites ridicule or derision of that which the satirist wills to mock.

Satire is a particularly capable agency for social control in any society where there is a fair consensus regarding its conventional values and standards. In the first place, as just noted, satire is the form of humor most concerned with comment on the norms of a society. It is probably the most specific and at the same time widespread and efficient use of humor and laughter in probing for and revealing deficiencies in the reigning norms, absurdities in the norms in the making, and foolish or socially questionable or dangerous departures from standard norms. Second, it functions as a powerful means of expressing public disapproval: universally feared, ridicule acts as a potent deterrent to deviant behavior. Third, satire is a way of effectively stating or implying what would be dangerous, or unwise, or embarrassing if presented directly; and it can act subtly. The satirist can say things which even the recognized reformer cannot easily or freely say. It may be much less difficult to laugh at the outrageous or evil person or group or situation than to discuss these objectively. Fourth, the bite of the criticism, the correction, and the punishment that satirical treatment can bring upon the deviant individual or collectivity is softened by the ensuing laughter, yet not weakened.[4]

3. PUBLIC HUMORISTS AS SOCIAL CRITICS AND CONTROLLERS

The public or semi-public and professional humorists are public in the sense of having a sizable impersonal audience to whom they make their appeal through literary, graphic, or electronic media of communication. In our day they consist of cartoonists, those producing satirical drawings, the writers of satirical or otherwise humorously critical novels and stories, the syndicated satirists and jokesmiths of our newspapers and journals, and the comedians, especially those of radio and television and the night clubs.

The public humorists have usually been critics of the social affairs of their day and age. They address themselves to political affairs (politics, politicians, parties and their proponents; political ideas, policies); to economic conditions and procedures; to particular social, especially, status groups, to manners and morals, to social philosophies, to social movements, and to all of the other aspects of human social life of wide concern which are vulnerable to humorous treatment.

---

[4] For what is still the definitive sociological treatment of satire see Lumley, 237-359. On the nature of satire and its social employment see also Carlisle, xiii-xvii; Dexter & White, 263-264; Elliott, 66-87; Swabey, 59-68; Winick, 1964: 276; Worcester, 8-9, 16, 34-37.

The humorists have in considerable part depended upon the aforementioned satire as a highly efficient technique for communicating their criticisms, and for instructing in what they have deemed to be the relevant and desirable political and social values, attitudes, norms, and practices.

Public humorists have played their revelationary and satirical role throughout history. Among the great ones of the past Aristophanes, Rabelais, Molière, Shakespeare, Cervantes, Swift, and Voltaire readily come to mind. There is the traditional or recurring Falstaff making bohemian, even obscene, sallies against the ins and their reputed decencies and their conformities.

The institutionalized jesters, including the public humorists of history, as their particular kind of critic, have performed certain functions in certain peculiar ways. First, as widely tolerated, even privileged, jesters they have been licensed to do things that other members of the society could not do with impunity. Second, in performing such functions, they have expressed and transmitted the potentially explosive discontent and criticism of many of the less articulate public and reduced the social pressure exercised by them. They have been referred to as safety-valve mechanisms and as lightning rods.

In our own United States public humorists have been among our most perspicacious critics and indirectly our keenest admonitors. A rich vein of especially satiric humor runs through our past, and there are some notable evidences of it in the present.

The nineteenth century produced a notable array of famous names. James Russell Lowell (1819–1891) in the sophisticated *Biglow Papers* satirized the war against Mexico and any extension of slave territory.

David Ross Locke (1833–1868), under the nom de plume Petroleum V. Nasby, was pro–Civil War on the Union side and dealt with those on the other side with caustic and corrosive irony.[5]

---

[5] See for example, the 720 pages of *The Struggles* (*Social, Financial, and Political*) *of Petroleum V. Nasby* (Boston: I. N. Richardson, 1872).

Charles Farrar Brown (1834–1867), also of the Civil War period, through his creation Artemus Ward, "the genial showman," made piercing satirical observations on the paradoxical affairs of the day in a bantering fashion which nevertheless constituted powerful criticism.

Thomas Nast (1840–1902) of the Gilded Age period, by means of his political cartoons in *Harper's Weekly,* conducted a campaign of caricature against various public characters and organizations. His cartoons played a notable part in exposing the financial shenanigans of the Tweed Ring in New York City and in bringing about the conviction of Boss (William M.) Tweed.

Ambrose Bierce (1842?–1914), with persistent satire and irony, blasted the ignorance, crudity, conceit, ill dress, bad manners, and general barbarity of the United States.

Mr. Dooley, famous character of Finley Peter Dunne (1867–1936) during the period of Cleveland, McKinley, Bryan, the war with Spain, and the first Roosevelt, through his comic comments, usually to "Mr. Hennessey," bore down not only on the political problems and politics and politicians of the day, but on other obvious and pressing social foibles and contradictions. Among other things, he uncovered "hollowness, sham and inhumanity in the high and mighty," the follies and indecencies of imperialism in the Philippines, "smug corruption, deceit, and lying in government and business," pretentious nonsense in education and religion, shady corporation lawyers, self-deified aristocrats, false theories and false reformers, and dishonest journalism (Beard, II, 439; Dudden, 29). This he did with jocose and waggish humor and rich satire.

Samuel L. Clemens (1835–1910), better known to us as Mark Twain, is sometimes referred to as America's greatest humorist. While political subjects elicited his righteous indignation, his robust humor and his satire ranged over a spectrum of mankind's faults far broader than politics alone. In *The Gilded Age* (1874)[6]

---

[6] Incidentally, this work provided the name which historians have given to the period of roughly 1865-1900.

(written in collaboration with Charles Dudley Warner) he lampooned the get-rich-quick mania and the corruption of government in the 1870's (the Grant administration). A theme which runs through adventure after adventure in *The Adventures of Huckleberry Finn* (1876) is man's indecency and cruelty to his fellowmen. Among the special targets against which he directed his criticism were the plutocrats, corrupt politicians, American mobs, and the sensational press. In general he bitterly criticized the past and contemporary follies and insufficiencies of what he came to think of as "the whole damned human race." And yet at the same time he showed a deep sympathy for the persons and institutions he was attacking.

The twentieth century has also supplied a number of outstanding humorous critical commentators upon the American scene.

Will Rogers (1879–1935), cowboy, actor, news commentator, and above all, crackerbox philosopher, for nearly the last two decades of his life functioned as "the nation's jester." With genial and homely but nonetheless piercing satire he reflected upon the American passing scene, applying himself to "everything from chewing gum to foreign affairs" (Beard, II, 771). The daily and widely demonstrated follies of the machine age came under his purview. Among other items, the pompous and not always so honorable big shots in Washington and Wall Street suffered his rapier thrusts, as did the narrow-minded, the blindly conventional, and the proudly mediocre. But Mr. Average Citizen also had many of his social absurdities and breaches gently but effectively ridiculed. Because of his sagacious wit "people laughed with him, and through him at themselves" (Dudden, 32).

Ring Lardner (1835–1933), sports writer, newspaper columnist, and writer of short stories, steered clear of politics for the most part; he admitted that he was unable to take politics seriously. His central interest, as he revealed it in his racy satirical pieces, was in the humorous characteristics and actions of folks in the ordinary walks of life—bellboys, policemen, housewives, salesmen, clerks, office girls, barbers, athletes, baseball players and their fans. He was specially given to exposing the antics of our city-dwelling culture-hounds and social climbers.

Henry L. Mencken (1880–1956), as editorial writer on the Baltimore *Sun* and as editor of the *Smart Set* and the *American Mercury*, raked the ways and institutions of his fellow Americans with withering scorn. While he probably was at his best lampooning politics, few aspects of our social life escaped his barbs. He especially poked vicious fun at the foibles of American democracy, such as its stupid complacency, its provincialism, its mob-like tendencies, and the ludicrous pretensions of many people to wisdom and sensibility (in brief, their existence as a "boobocracy") and such other features as boosterism, fundamentalism, puritanism, and prohibition. No institution, no social class, no person, and no idea was spared from his raillery and derison.

James G. Thurber (1894–1961), writer and artist with the *New Yorker* from 1927 on, is considered by some to be the best American humorist since Mark Twain. His medium was his satirical books and articles illustrated with his inimitable cartoons. He occupied himself mainly with the small events of everyday life: the odd actions of people in different kinds of situations, the amusing aspects of the war between the sexes, the daily pretensions and evasions of people. But there was often the hint that these opened up wide vistas and larger horizons. He had a keen satirical sense, but it was tempered by a gentle humor. (See especially Mikes, 107–125.)

In recent decades we have also had Helen Hokinson (1893–1949) lampooning club-women stuffiness by her drawings in the *New Yorker* and the other sophisticated satirical drawings and cartoons in the *New Yorker* and the *Saturday Review;* Westbrook Pegler (1894–1969) with his scornfully derisive denunciations and exposures in his comments upon the news and in his sardonically funny stories; Peter Arno (1904—) gently and subtly satirizing human types and ways by means of his drawings; the penetratingly revelatory and often denunciatory exposition of persons, institutions, events, and relationships of public concern by Bill Mauldin (1921—), Herblock (1909—), and others in their cartoons. The reader is also aware of Chaplin, Don Marquis, Robert Benchley, the Marx Brothers (especially Groucho), Ogden Nash, Clarence Day, Dorothy Parker, E. B. White, S. J. Perelman, Jack Benny, Fred Allen, Bob Hope, Red Skelton, Mort Sahl and others, each operating in his own special genre.

A new luminary among the public humorists is Art Buchwald (1925—). He has a tremendous contact with the public through his syndicated column and is considered by many to be the funniest of contemporary American newspaper columnists and one of the sharpest and widely heeded political satirists. He is squarely in the tradition of our great newspaper satirists of the past. With satire, exaggeration in some instances, overplaying in others, and sly innuendo, he fearlessly brings out the logical and factual absurdities and perversions of a wide range of public situations and personages, from politicians to Supreme Court justices, and from race relations to auto driving in Tokyo.

These public humorist critics and satirists have been, in some measure, agents of social revision and innovation as well as comic reviewers of things as they are. In general, they have aligned themselves against foolish or patently harmful deviations from custom, decency, or good sense. They have especially torn the masks off public figures who have tried to conceal questionable enterprises, and have devastatingly revealed their shenanigans. They have done the same for organizations and institutions responsible for the conditions they reveal. What is more, they have held up a mirror in which the individual or collective culprits see themselves as they actually are in their foolishness and transgression and put them on the defensive. They have disclosed and castigated the big and little stultifying lies and myths of our national life. In considerable measure they have functioned as the conscience of the country. Their criticisms have often suggested that control, or some modification of control of a corrective nature in the areas of social life exposed by them was desirable, even urgent. Their role thus has been that of *agents provocateurs* of essential forms of social control, and of necessary greatly revised or new social conditions. The fear of attention from the public humorists has doubtless prevented many a stupid, indecent, or illegal act.

The social criticism of a few of them has been presented in a bitterly derisive, caustic, even brutal manner, notably "Petroleum V. Nasby," Ambrose Bierce, and Henry L. Mencken. But most of them have criticized the grave social situation in a playful, genial, sympathetic, even compassionate fashion. By the laughter they have aroused they have headed off not only tears but also debilitating rage.[7]

4. HUMOR AND LAUGHTER IN AMERICAN ADVERTISING

Humor and laughter are both positively and negatively involved in American advertising.

A. On the positive side is the use of humor (and the related laughter) as a means of social control; specifically, as an aid in persuading the public to buy the particular commodity or service. It is resorted to as one of the advertiser's subtleties along with flattery, argument, coaxing, half-truths. It has several useful aspects. The witty phrase or idea or graphic incident portrayed may serve as an attention getter. There is also the appeal to the sense of humor of the targets as the attempt is made to transfer into comic situations the functions or the products of the advertiser. The humorous procedure of course is intended to create a friendly and favorable attitude toward the commodity or service reinforced by the euphoria of laughter. What is sought is conversion by humor.

The humorous appeal is found occasionally in the advertisements transmitted by most of the mass media—newspapers, periodicals, radio, television. In the journals we find such devices as the eye-catching droll small child dressed in adult clothing; the jocular situation involving a group of five or six persons as

---

[7] On American public humorists as social critics and controllers see Beard, Bier, Blair, Dudden, Harris, Thorp, Weber, Yates. For some of the wider social implications of their humor see Masson, Foreword.

the setting for the advertising plea; the cigarette smoker with the black eye announcing "That's why us Tareyton smokers would rather fight than switch." There is special resort to a humorous play on words: Ronrico Rum suggesting "Try it. You have nothing Toulouse"; the different kinds of Campbell's soups as "The Manhandlers"; the firm making Monroe Calculators boosting their sales and service principles as "The Monroe Doctrine."

Occasional unique usages are found such as window advertising signs employed by local retail establishments in a Nebraska community. A maternity shop advised, "We Provide the Accessories After the Fact." A meat market presented itself as "Your friendly used-cow dealer." An Italian restaurant inquired, "Have you tangled with our spaghetti?" A loan company announced, "We serve the man who has everything . . .but hasn't paid for it."

A surprising aspect of this humor and laughter in advertising, however, in the light of its demonstrated positive efficacy in many social situations, is the limited degree in which it is used. Most advertisements are deadly serious. It would seem that either (1) the advertising agencies have not discovered humor and laughter as valuable "natural resources" with vast technological possibilities or (2) they have concluded that humor has a limited and declining appeal in the contemporary American setting, at least as an aid in extracting wealth from people.

B. More evident than the intentional efforts to control the potential purchasing public by humor in advertising is the unintentional blocking of control due to the repellent content and/or form of presenting some of it. This is especially the case with some radio and television advertisements. These arouse in the targets the laughter of sardonic amusement or even hostility. This laughter is provoked by the ridiculousness of some of the terms used, for example, when taken from other and irrelevant areas of life. Or the laughter at the preposterousness of the claims made, namely, that one does not act intelligently and cannot be healthy, happy, secure, or socially acceptable unless he buys the products in question. The method of delivery may arouse antagonism: the rasping or strident voices, the shouting, the insipid dialogue. There may be critical laughter about the advertisements in and of themselves: their frequency, their length, their repetition, their exaggeration, not infrequently their misrepresentation obvious to the most unsophisticated of their audience, their absurdity, their mawkish sentimentality, or otherwise obnoxious nature. Instead of willing yielding there is a powerful motivation to turn it off!

X. Laughter and Social Change

Social change is a widely inclusive term—the generic designation for all societary modification. More specifically, it consist in alterations of societal structures, of patterns of social behavior and relationship, of social positions and conditions of population elements, of social functions and processes. As in change in general, causation is always involved. Social change, of course, may be permanent or temporary, and beneficial or harmful in its effects; it may be planned or unplanned and unidirectional or multidirectional.

1. THE GENERAL PLACE OF LAUGHTER IN SOCIAL CHANGE

Laughter is a factor in social change, both as effect and as cause. In the discussion of laughter in its temporal context (chap. v, sec. 5) the close relationship between laughter and change was brought out. The facts and principles there presented have direct relevance to the present chapter. With social change there *is* a change in laughter-inducing situations and in laughter themes as was noted with special reference to jokes as reflectors of the era and as timely provocatives of laughter. In the immediately preceding chapter we were concerned with laughter as a social control agent, involving its significance both in the positive preservation of social order and *pari passu* the avoidance of anti-social change, and as a spur to change in the way of corrective action.

The present chapter addresses itself to another basic aspect of the relationship between laughter and social change: namely, with the circumstances, capacities, functions, and effects of laughter in blocking and in effecting changes in social ideas, attitudes, codes, organizations, and institutions. The general principle is that the humorous reactions of individuals and groups, overtly expressed in their laughter, are a dynamic factor in activating them, and thus, as they act, in reducing or producing social change. The specific principle is that, under varying social circumstances, people perceive the status quo differently. There is, on their part, an awareness of incongruity between what is and what is wanted and what is objected to that provokes their laughter. By it they may confirm and applaud the status quo in some areas or "theaters" of interest and criticize and condemn the departures from the status quo or the changes recommended or attempted. In other cases they may protest against or criticize the status quo by their hostile laughter and provide a strong incentive to change.

Two important aspects of the part that laughter plays in the social change of the group, community, or society stand out: (1) its conservative and conservational functions and effects as these contribute to the maintenance of the status quo, and (2) its effectiveness as a renovative-reorganizational aid in keeping the collectivity functionally effective through time.

2. CONSERVATIVE AND CONSERVATIONAL FUNCTIONS AND EFFECTS

In certain aspects of its performance in some social situations laughter is resistant to social changes. This is especially true of it in its disciplining role. This role is pointedly revealed in laughter's closely related conservative and conservational effects. Distrust not only of the deviant but especially of the new and atypical and unusual, and respect for the customary, the traditional, the prevailing, the accepted, is responsible for this function of laughter. We laugh at strange people, strange speech, strange customs; we laugh at many of the new ideas and ways and forms which have not yet become accepted and stabilized elements of our experience and standard in our life routines. This is the laughter which attacks extravagances and eccentricities and confirms things as they are, which points to seemingly preposterous suggested changes along many lines, which saves us from pollution by the untried, and which is, up to a point, an essential of stability and safety. But it may also kill the germs of variation, and as its extreme effect may preserve social rigidity, and be obstructive of social well-being and societal efficacy. It is common knowledge, for example, that the laughter of the crowd has slowed up the first use of hosts of practical inventions as well as new ideas that later have had a wide reign.

By means of this laughter, change is signaled and challenged. Startling newfangled ideas in almost any department of life (including ethics and religion, and in some cases even science); departures from the established or prevailing manners, morals, fashions, or many of the ordinary usages and utilities of life; fads in many areas of behavior; many innovations in institutional forms and ways; many new technological inventions; most social prophets, pioneers and reformers; most new social movements; and occasionally new public personages—these are the targets of malicious mirth.

Many of us laugh at the rebellion of individuals against even some of the most hollow of conventions, which, as even the most moderate of rebels will agree to, tends to keep them in line.

In general, what more or less violently jars with the long-standing and the existent is at least at first often the legitimate game for ridiculing laughter.

It is especially significant that such critical laughter is a warning that must be heeded by those who would suggest or attempt novelties or even next steps. It acts as a testing device as it makes the new ideas, and ways, and gadgets, and organizations, and movements prove themselves. Laughter at the strange and new does not stop until the innovation has quite generally demonstrated its validity and utility.

Such laughter, of course, also helps to sustain what has been valued; it helps to maintain the social regularities; it protects the mores and the institutions from the sudden or premature intrusion of alien or untried ways; it functions as a guard against corruption or inundation by "foreigners" or "aliens" or "dangerous people." It has a preservative effect on culture and society (Sully, 256–258, 280–281; Sidis, 30, 38–40; Lumley, 276–279; Duncan, 1953: 51; Piddington, 148).

In the last analysis, laughter as a conservative agent has its ultimate effect on the individual. If he swings out too far in dress, or speech, or extreme behavior of any kind, the laughter of his fellows engulfs him and often chastens him. But there is a broader social aspect. Social laughter often is an expression of criticism, even outrage, by the herd against the maverick, or the independent. As such it tends to persuade the individual to abide by the average, the stereotyped, and the widely accepted of time and place.

3. THE RENOVATIVE-REORGANIZATIONAL FUNCTIONS AND EFFECTS

A converse function and effect of derisive laughter as a conservative-conservational factor is its effectiveness as a renovative-reorganizational agent. At first glance these opposite features would seem to imply inconsistency; actually, however, both forms may be and often are engaged in by different population segments with respect to the same situation, and possibly by the same population segments at different times; for example, at different developmental stages of a particular social phenomenon.

This renovative function is that of the ridiculing, cynical, or skeptical laughter which routs out and parodies and criticizes worn-out or false ideas, and beliefs, and ideologies, repressive or restrictive social codes, outmoded or stereotyped proprieties and ways of life, archaic or petrified institutional forms, organizational rigidities, inelasticities of habit, customs, conventions, rituals and ceremonies, shams and superstitions, stupid rigamaroles, hidden absurdities, stuffy solemnity, "fundamentalism," overconformity, and formalism—not to mention all manner of outmoded physical machines and techniques. Critical humor, employing the various laughter-evoking devices, is widely resorted to as a means of revealing sick spots and dead ends and hardening of the arteries—of showing up what is wrong.

This renovative laughter is directed at certain types of individuals as well as certain sociocultural conditions. It focuses its criticism and ridicule not only on the social and moral deviants of various kinds mentioned in the previous chapter but also on diehards, reactionaries, and many overconformers. It ferrets out old fogies.

This is laughter not as social prophylaxis—to be examined in Chapter XII—but as social purgative. It is the laughter that helps to remove the useless, the unprofitable, the outworn—the laughter that "helps to give the *coup de grâce* to mere baggage" (Lumley, 283).

Such laughter pursues a utilitarian aim of general improvement and functions as a check on social rigidity, social decadence, and social obsolescence. It is a means of overcoming paralyzing resistances to essential change and of reducing sociocultural and societal stresses and strains. It favors flexibility and innovation and exerts pressure to invent. It has demonstrated itself historically in every great period and movement of change, for example the Reformation, the Renaissance, and the English and French revolutions. Social reformers have resorted to it as an effective weapon.

An important aspect of the laughter that is renovative-reorganizational is that it *is* critical, and implies that the laughers at least suggest some reformation; for example, the laughter at or about the prohibition laws and their violation, the laughter at "crazy monstrosities" in painting and sculpture, the cynical laughter at the release by the courts of another confessed criminal, or the light fine imposed on the politically protected public servant found guilty of crimes against the public.

Several facts stand out by way of conclusion. First, laughter fuctions as a potent influence on the social functionaries that in some measure, by virtue of their position, roles, and functions, manipulate social change: the leaders of social movements, the elites, the inventors in the different departments of life, the organizational administrators. Second, laughter is a factor in the actions of groups and communities as they seek to make effective their strain toward adjustment and the continuous restoration of equilibrium in their physical, psychosocial, and societal environments. Third, laughter, by checking too rapid and radical change on the one hand and the sway of persistent and repressive archaisms on the other, tends to aid in maintaining a sort of equilibrium between the extremes and as such functions as a guarantor of optimal change.

XI. Laughter in the Status System

Laughter performs a variety of functions in the operation of the status systems of groups, communities, and societies. Some of these functions are in sharp contrast to each other, as is brought out in the first two major divisional topics of the present chapter, namely, laughter as social equalizer or leveler on the one hand and as maintainer of status differences and levels on the other. The third involves class differences in laughter behavior.

1. LAUGHTER AS SOCIAL EQUALIZER OR LEVELER

Laughing together on the part of occupants of the different statuses may have a distinct equalizing effect, and is often resorted to in order to bring about at least a temporary feeling, possibly even state, of equality. Laughing together across status lines, at least for the moment, unblocks communication between the unequals and is a release from the sense of difference of rank and the disaffection due to status differentiation. Social barriers are pushed into the background, social space is diminished, and the divisiveness of horizontal as well as vertical distance is reduced. This tendency is apt to prevail between representatives of the different social classes, the ranks of organizations, employer and employees, dean and lowly instructor; between members of ethnic, age, and sex groups.

Joined laughter, however, does not eliminate or ignore or hide social distances and differentials. It is simply a sort of signal of safety between the unequals. A temporary common social climate relatively free from status sensitiveness is created; momentary accommodation, possibly reciprocity, on a common plane prevails.

The joined laughter evidences a common joy, or delight with a common humorous situation, or a common success or triumph. In general, he "who invites others to laugh with him creates or strengthens the feeling of equality in the participants" (Coser, 1959: 177). The very action of laughing together is a show of equality and a feat of leveling.[1]

Very different is the effective use of laughter as equalizer of social power between the social classes or levels, it being obvious, of course, that the upper levels usually have a disproportionate amount of power. The socially powerless can at least exercise the power of protest against the inequality of power by means of their critical, their defiant, even their demonic, laughter at the powerful. But it can be much more, since in effect it is in some measure a denial by the weak and lowly of the power of the societal power holders, a de-idolizing of them, an exorcising of their ideology, a victory over them.

2.   LAUGHTER IN THE MAINTENANCE OF EXISTENT STATUS DIFFERENCES AND LEVELS

There is much laughter by those involved in status relations, however, which does not function as a facilitator of communication, a shrinker of social distances, or an effector of social-status equality. We now note that inability to laugh together, whether unintentional due to blocks to communication of a psychological, cultural, or societal nature between representatives of different social classes or levels of the hierarchy of organizations, or intentional refusal to laugh together, or the direction of derisive laughter against the other class (or classes) or organizational stratum is a factor in maintaining status differences and levels. Also, a differential order of permissiveness regarding laughter in

---

[1] On laughter as equalizer see also Coser, 1960: 81, 87-88, 95; Duncan, 1955: 54-55.

the different types of inter-status relationships seems to prevail among the representatives of the different statuses.

A. In a community or society where there are sharp cultural differences between ethnic or majority-minority groups, or between classes or castes, these differences may function as blocks to communication. The various population segments may be so different in cultural conditioning that given situations are not funny or otherwise laughable to all of them and hence are not conducive to joined laughter. Also, they do not always laugh *at* the same things, since the things, or conditions, or actions which they oppose and ridicule are different.

B. Some of those in the upper-status levels seem to make a distinct effort to avoid laughing with social class inferiors or lower level persons in their organizational hierarchies as a means of maintaining their status distinction, at least in their own eyes. There is, for example, the occasional petty "superior" in a bureaucracy who resents "inferiors" freely laughing with him as an affront to his dignity and position.

On the other hand, the joined laughter *within* an upper stratum or otherwise (possibly self-appointed) prestigious segment is not only a unifier among the members but functions especially as a means of self-assurance, even self-flattery. It is possible that many readers of the rather pretentious *New Yorker*, as they enjoy its humor, have "the illusion of belonging to an aloof, sophisticated, esoteric, and fastidious minority," "an aristocracy of brains and culture" (Worcester, 77).

C. Derisive laughter against other status levels, whether directed up or down the status structure, calls attention to sharp differences of viewpoint, concern, in some cases jealousies, even antipathies, between the levels. Often it reflects the dissociation inherent in the status system. It maintains the social distances and the inequalities between "superiors" and "inferiors." It can have the effect of erecting floors between the levels. When exercised by the lower status elements, it may express rebellion against the power of the upper statuses; and when performed by the upper levels may show an air of superiority and give indication to the lower class persons to stay in their place. It may be used by the upper-stratum elements to justify and sustain their advantaged position.

There is, however, the occasional instance in inter-status relations (for example, between races) of the manipulation of laughter among the lesser ranks by those in power—in curtailing their own derisive laughter or in inducing joined laughter—to prevent disaffection from taking dangerous forms. It may well be, owing to the very nature of the status system, that the ameliorative laughter for easing the status tensions must come downward from the upper levels.

This laughing at or against incumbents of other status levels may also function as a means of exposing the worst excesses of hierarchy. Each level may do so by humorously or contemptuously joking about the position of the other, or about identifying characteristics, or typical behavior of the other side. Outsiders, by means of jokes, cartoons, and satirical portrayals, may gently or viciously lampoon one level or the other at its more vulnerable points.

At the same time the suppressive laughter and the laughter directed against the uppers by the lower-class levels, the incumbents of the lower organizational layers, the members of demeaned social, ethnic, nationality, or religious minorities is for these "lesser" social elements, a psychical escape from their suppressed and unequal estate.

D.   Social interaction in any group or society requires some degree of consensus among its constitutive elements; that is, mutually accepted definitions of situations and shared norms of behavior regarding those situations, if the social structure is to operate effectively. This principle applies among the incumbents of the different levels of status systems. There must be a certain compatibility between the role players in the different statuses.

In all societies laughter, as induced by joking or playful banter, is a short cut to consensus between incumbents of different statuses. The joking relationship provides a double understanding that permits the contemporaneous maintenance of the different status positions. This is explicitly revealed in hierarchical organizations like factories and armies.

While in effect the representatives of the respective statuses may victimize each other with friendly ridicule of banter, they share in it and are participants in a common unit of action. Also, while the banter is shared in a manner connoting goodwill and friendliness, each status participates in it at the expense of the other. Each maintains the exclusiveness of his status, and the status pattern is not damaged. In effect, they have agreement regarding their status relationship. This agreement accepts the status arrangement, safeguards the relationship between the representatives as they play their respective parts in the different but interrelated positions, and assures peaceful, amicable inter-action.

The joking relationship thus is a modus operandi which implies consensus regarding the status system, and which contributes to its effective operation as this involves the inter-status personal relations. The respective statuses are protected without disrupting the general social organization in which the statuses are involved. Finally, it enables the representatives of the statuses not only to get along together but also to cooperate as they perform their roles.[2]

E. What people laugh at regarding the behavior of aspirants to higher status indicates at the same time what is essential or valid in the status allocation. The hopefully upwardly mobile who seek acceptance in a higher stratum thus are confronted with the possibility of laughter, especially the threat of being laughed at, as a sharp device for challenging and checking upon their suitability and their competence to fulfill the demands of the higher status and its roles. Here the laughter functions as a facilitator of communication, but with critical, and not leveling or welcoming, intent. Among the aspirants there always are the upstarts, the fourflushers, the phonies, the too-eager beavers, the braggarts, the bunk shooters, the glad-handers, and the apple polishers. By means of the laughter at them by both the top dogs, the ins, the established, and the general

---

[2] This section has been suggested by and is in part derived from Burns, 656-657.

observers of the status system (including lower level incumbents), the behaviors of these are pinpointed, and their claims
and qualifications are scrutinized and kept in check. All aspirants of course, to meet the test of laughter must, as we put it,
show their stuff and have what it takes. The false and/or incompetent claimants are thus deflated (cut down to size), scared
out, and quite likely, kept out. Laughter also may be a device
for pruning the status structure of deceitful climbers and am-
bitious small-timers. Furthermore, since people do not want to
be laughed at, the critical laughter helps to keep people in that
niche with which their abilities are most compatible.

However, it is not uncommon to find some well-established
and well-protected incumbents of upper strata laughed at as
snobs, stuffed shirts, playboys, or parasites—which they occasionally are. It might be noted in passing that some of the most
telling American humor has been an expression of irreverence
toward the incumbents of the higher statuses of our society.

F.   As implied before, a sort of "pecking order" in interpersonal laughter seems to prevail between the representatives of
the different strata in the inter-status relationships. Some smiling
and laughing, according to the situation, can be considered to
be unconscious or conscious nonverbal communicative signaling
having to do with the differential behavior of the various levels
of incumbents with each other in the social hierarchy and in
aggressive-submissive interactions; specifically, communication
about peck-order matters. The laughter particularly indicates
who can laugh at whom in what specific types of structural relations and sociocultural situations.[3]

In general, humor and the related laughter in a hierarchically
ordered social structure tends to be directed downward. The
uppers are more likely to set the humor pace. First, it seems that
initiative in creating joined laughter as a utilitarian unifier or
expediter in a social situation usually comes from above. For
example, the initiative in the use of humor to reduce social

---

[3] Much of this section is drawn from or has been suggested by Coser,
1960; 1966. On the pecking order among laughers see also Fry, 90-111.

distance (or in some smaller measure to contribute to equalization) is usually by the senior or "superior" members in the hierarchical system; in fact, initiative by the status-superior seems to be expected. This conforms to the principle set forth by Homans (145): "A person of higher social rank than another originates interaction for the latter more often than the latter originates interaction for him."

Ordinarily, it is more permissible for the senior staff member in the authority structure, or the member of the upper class in the stratification structure, than for someone lower to laugh first in a given humorous situation; the lesser then may join it.

In laughing *at* members of other levels, those who are on top in the hierarchy have more "right" in most situations to engage in aggressive or critical laughter than do the lesser levels. Those lower down on the totem pole do not feel so free to make witticisms or to indulge in laughter directed against higher-level representatives. In fact, they feel that in most such situations to do so is risky. Coser (1960; 85) points out that the failure of those in subordinate levels of the hierarchical system to use their wit is not necessarily a reflection on their ability or their character, but is rather a submission to the demands of the social structure. Among the hospital staff studied by Coser the most frequent targets of the senior staff were junior members, whose humor or laughter in turn was more often directed against patients and their relatives, as well as against themselves (85). At the same time the lowers or juniors have to bear with being laughed at by the superiors.

Juniors in hierarchies, lower-class members, and members of minority ethnic groups, can and often do ingratiate themselves with status superiors by offering themselves as the butt of upper-stratum humor. They may also thus protect themselves against active aggression on the part of the superiors. Laughing at some intentionally comic antic of the superior is often a means of currying favor with him. As the pertinent quip goes: "Nothing improves a joke more than when it is told by the boss." Similarly, it seems to be a general principle that only equals can laugh with or at each other without challenging or disturbing status-system relationships and amenities. An ancient Djabo proverb states, "One teases another only if one is equal to him."

G.   Another important aspect of laughter in the status structure—in a sense involving the other side of the pecking-order shield—is the seeming fact that when group laughter is directed against an individual, its significance depends on the social prominence or weight of the target in the group or society. The socially eminent or conspicuous person, by virtue of his position in government or politics, in religion, in commerce or industry, in public entertainment, or even in crime is more likely to be the subject of such laughter and more likely to be affected by it than socially inconspicuous or otherwise less important persons. The laughter is thus a sort of social control over the big shots.

H.   The social managers, aware of the disruptive potency of reciprocally aggressive laughter of status levels against each other, realize that a certain amount of manipulation of laughter is desirable in the interests of social well-being and stability. They, as the ones in power, must themselves know how to laugh, as well as how to be safely laughed at, without suffering embarrassment or reduction or impairment of rank. They must know that the engendering of laughter of mirth or friendliness across rank lines is a desirable device to hold down aggression against the status system from any rank. They also must know that joined laughter with or at a common object of ridicule or aggression is an effective way of draining off disruptive status feeling. They should know in tense situations how to find *safe* things to laugh about jointly and to recognize that the proper manipulation of such inciters to laughter is an important task of social management.[4]

3. DIFFERENTIALS IN LAUGHTER BEHAVIOR BETWEEN THE SOCIAL STRATA

It has long been recognized that what the members of the different social strata experience in identical situations, what

---

[4] On laughter as a factor in reducing strains between faculty and students in a nurses' training school see Olesen & Whittaker. On the relation of humor and roles and statuses see Coser, 1966.

they perceive mentally and socially, what they respond to, and what they do may differ very considerably. This is reflected in some of the differences in what they laugh at or about, and also the amount and form of their laughter. This, of course, relates somewhat to the influence of education and cultural and social socialization and sophistication in producing differences in their laughter behavior.

A. It has been noted that there is some difference as to sensitivity to certain niceties and decencies regarding bodily functions. Warner (34), for example, some years ago called attention to the differing attitude regarding excretory and sexual functions between the different social levels of "Yankee City." While all men are equal regarding these functions, he noted that the functions were not equally stressed as interests by the different classes, nor was the humorous attitude toward them similar. He summarized: "Scatological humor plainly styled and openly stated, although accepted and sometimes appreciated by the higher levels, is most enjoyed by the lower extreme of American life. The superior classes are most likely to respond to subtle sexual jokes, less to bluntly told sexual ones, and least to anal ones where the humor largely depends on explicit and conscious use of fecal symbols."

Such class differentials are also observed with respect to other areas in which prevailing conceptions of decency of the community impose limits and taboos. (Cf. chap. xv, sec. 3.)

Important is the fact that an upper-class person who acts unseemly regarding such decried or tabooed laughter behavior may not only invite the criticism or disdain of many of his class associates, but may even declass himself.

B. It has also been observed that there are differences between the social classes with respect to the restraints they tend to impose upon different degrees of laughter itself. The more cultivated upper strata are likely to be more restrained in their laughter in most social situations than those of the lower strata. Though intellectually stimulated by the humorous incident, they control their emotional expression. They are inclined to express their pleasure, or enthusiasm, or friendliness, or mirth by smiles rather than by laughter, by the slight subtle humorous gesture of hand or eyebrow as against the uncouth body rumble.

Many upper-class persons are embarrassed by sturdy guffaws on the part of fellow class members, for example at a play or almost any social gathering. They are likely to look upon boisterous or even hearty laughter as undignified or uncouth.

XII. Laughter as a
Social Therapeutic Agent

Some of the functions of laughter as engaged in by the individual to maintain himself as a person among his associates were examined in Chapter VI, section 2. We now point to some of the specific *social* therapeutic and cathartic functions performed by social laughter, in both its repressive and aggresive forms, in different types of tense or unhealthy social situations in collectivities. This includes the laughter of the joined group members as a social tonic, as a sustaining factor when suffering adversity, as a means of coping with the forbidden, as an easer of social tensions, as a means of adjusting to group failure or infirmity, as a means of enduring tyranny and subjugation.

1. LAUGHING TOGETHER AS A TONIC AND LIFT

In general, laughing together by members of a group has been a refreshing tonic of considerable value for them in maintaining mental and societal health. Not only is tension demobilized as the laughter drains off safely and even delightfully what has been too rigid or routine, or depressive, or repressive; in the process the members often receive a new freedom and expansiveness. The joined laughter suffuses them with a feeling of well-being; it restores and enlivens and brightens them. Group tone is heightened. (Cf. Sully, 415–417; Montagu, 1960: 32.)

2. LAUGHING TOGETHER IN ADVERSITY
AND AT OPPRESSORS

Laughing together on the part of members of collectivities suffering adverse conditions has been a sustaining factor through the ages. This has been especially noticeable in the case of pioneers suffering the hardships of the frontier, both soldiers at the front and civilians at home in wartime, ethnic and social minorities subjugated and exploited by the majority, slave laborers, prisoners, the victims of tyrannies and dictatorships. For example, in our American history the pioneers and backwoodsmen needed to adjust to their harsh conditions. Their laughter gave them resilience in meeting their many unaccustomed obstacles and a sense of triumph over them. (Rourke, 98–99.) In wartime, humor aids in living with the conditions of war. Bairnsfather's cartoons in World War I and Mauldin's in World War II, in finding humor in war's bleakest situations, assuaged people's sorrows and worries, and to some extent, kept them from heartbreak.

Often in a tense dominator-dominated situation, the disadvantaged, the confined, the oppressed, the exploited, the condemned, have also obtained some relief from laughing *at* those responsible for their plight. In most instances it has been the victims laughing *with* each other wherever they had any kind of communication with each other as they laughed at the controllers and the socially favored.

3. "GALLOWS HUMOR" AND THE UNFREE

Suppressive laughter is especially effective in relieving tension in the areas of social life where the people involved do not have the opportunity to express themselves freely and openly, or in areas where behavior is very strictly regulated. Pertinent are the "gallows humor" and the closely related "comic obscenity" with their accompanying laughter. Gallows humor is the savage and often also obscene humor of the sufferers of precarious or dangerous situations. Those causing the situation are ridiculed with irony, invective, and sarcasm. Gallows humor provides an escape from, or a means of living with, horror and death: the humor and laughter of the concentration camps, of death row, of soldiers at the front. It is a prime means of keeping up and strengthening the morale and the spirit of resistance of the victims in their struggle for survival; it is not only a manifestation of their morale, but also a reliable index of it. A very important aspect of it, as someone has put it, is that it functions as "a weapon of the mind in the struggle for its preservation."[1]

4. A DEFENSE AGAINST THREATS

Joking and laughter are resorted to by collectivities as well as by individuals as a means of defense against the threatening aspects of situations. Mechanic observes that students in a state of stress as they anticipate examinations often joke about their predicament. They use humor to avoid thinking about the more serious possibilities of the anxiety-provoking matter.

5. LAUGHTER AS A MEANS OF COPING WITH THE FORBIDDEN

Humor and the related laughter enable people to live with some of the most insistently tabooed realities of human life, however sinister, awesome, fearsome, obscene, indelicate, or contrary to the reigning conventions they may be believed to be. Some of the taboos are the effects of social prejudice. Humor with its independent spirit frequently challenges and criticizes some of these prejudices—often prejudices connected with aspects of life that are in themselves natural, normal, and essential. Various humorous devices weaken or soften these prejudices and enable the human beings involved to live with the taboos.

A. While not all euphemisms—"nice," or "dry-cleaned," or otherwise more agreeable terms for the description of disagreeable or proscribed concepts, conditions, occurrences, or things—are humorous, a considerable number are. Such euphemisms by their humor and the laughter they generate make the conventionally ominous realities to which they refer less reprehensible.[2]

---

[1] The classic treatment of gallows humor is that of Obrdlik. See also Duncan, 1962: 407-411.

[2] On controlling awesome, obscene, indelicate situations in general by euphemisms see J. O. Hertzler, *A Sociology of Language* (N. Y.: Random House, 1965), 276-279, 298. On euphemisms as humorous linguistic devices see sec. 2B, D, below.

B.   Comic obscenity provides forms of relaxation of the more or less constant taboos imposed by the society on the discussion of some human anatomical features and on sexual (erotic) and scatological (excrementitious) behavior. Comic obscenity eases the naughtiness of the acts as the laughers laugh about them together. It is also a way of overcoming shock and terror. Furthermore, obscene humor makes evil laughable, and this, in turn, enables the laughers to live with evil. The comic obscenity of the soldier, for example, is a means of living with the fear of the possible attack, the possibility of death, with bad food, filth, weather, abnormal social life.[3]

C.   It is worthy of special reference that laughter offers ways of living with sex in a fairly acceptable and equable manner. Historically in our culture reference to sex has been a more or less forbidden thing. Some of this long-standing attitude still lingers on. Sex still cannot be treated openly in some social circles; to speak of it freely is to encourage rebuke. Yet there is the almost universal preoccupation with it. The outlawing of the ever-present and ever-pressing sexual life by society provides a standing opportunity for a usually playful defiance of the code regarding it, and the allusion to it or the joking about it is an invitation to oppose the taboo. The almost certain joined laughter softens possible embarrassment and reduces the feelings of guilt that some of the company might have about sex. Even more importantly, this laughter provides the satisfying and socially acceptable expression of the lawless spirit prevailing among the conspirators. It is also often a socially safe, or at least blame-diluted, form of rebellion against the constraints imposed on sex.[4]

---

[3] On obscene wit see Freud, 138-145; Flugel, 719-720; Duncan, 1962: 407-411.

[4] For what amounts to a concise historical inventory of the literature of erotics, with particular reference to collections of erotic and scatological jokes and tales see Legman. While he points out that cultures have differed from each other, and given cultures have differed at different times with respect to their attitude toward erotic humor, he also indicates that sexual humor has been a normal part of the humor and life of most peoples.

In recent decades the attitude toward sex has liberalized markedly in the United States and most other modernized countries. Not only have the taboos against acknowledged interest in sex and upon the open and public discussion of sexual behavior and relations weakened in many quarters, but there has been a marked swing toward devotion to sex and a wanton display of sex even to the extent of public performance of sexual intercourse in avant garde motion pictures, plays, and esthetic dances. Instead of there being surreptitious laughter as an out against social and artistic restraints upon sex, the laughter in many mod circles is that directed *against* those who are square or old-hat about sex.

D. With laughter one can often get away with what could be dangerous actions and reactions. This is exemplified in the warning, "Laugh, damn you, when you say that!"

To see the comic in a situation and to laugh about it is a good antidote against panic. Furthermore, to produce laughter is sometimes a way of dispelling panic.

Delicate or ambiguous relationships are often eased by laughter. Mother-in-law jokes serve almost classically to vent feelings of antagonism in sons-in-law. Laughter may even be a means of living with some of the ceaseless horrors of life, such as death on the highways.

6. LAUGHTER AS EASER OF SOCIAL SITUATIONS

A. It can be presented as a general proposition that laughing at the repressors or restrainers is an expression of the itching of people to turn on their manipulators, regulators, those regimenting them; for example, the jokes directed at bosses, masters, clergymen, prison guards, dictators.

B. Closely related is the laughter which comes as a reaction against the repressive forces of society in general: the galling pressures of institutions, mores, conventions, rules, proprieties, refinements, regularities, organizational requirements, taboos, etcetera. Such laughter, however, is more than an expression cf irritation. It is a chance to rebel a bit, even though vicariously.

It is something desirable now and then, possibly even a social necesity. As it has been variously put (Patrick, 107-108, 114, 122; Lumley, 284), it is for the affected participants, a means of blowing off steam, a shock absorber, a social safety valve, a vacation from customary or conventional suppressions, a momentary rebellion against or escape from social oppressions and rigors, a formal release from the constant galling grip or tyranny of social claims and restraints. It is especially significant in conflict situations. For example, as labor and management sit around the table when a strike is threatened, laughter at a pat joke may drain off hostile and aggressive sentiments, and prevent probable conflict or reduce its disruptive effects.

Jokes also play a part in overcoming repression such as G. I. jokes about the brass, or the above-mentioned sex jokes. The laughter is like nose-thumbing at authority, and represents a sort of victory of the laugher over the suppression by the group or society.

Many societies have had special and periodic occasions or intervals given in part at least to more or less institutionalized fun-making and mild licentiousness, even topsy-turvydom. These fun festivals exemplify the universal communal recognition of the desirability of humor, merrymaking, joy, gaiety and mirth on the one hand, and the at least temporary release from the somberness, stodginess, austerity, and routine of daily existence, as well as from the galling social regulations and taboos. They are times of free fun and chartered license. In ancient Rome the Bacchanalia, the festival in honor of Bacchus, was given to drunken orgies. The Lupercalia, occurring February 15, glorified the rustic deity Lupercus with revelries. The Saturnalia, extending from December 17 to December 24, and commemorating the peaceful reign of Saturn, was a period of carnival, a festival of feasting and drinking, of general joy and unrestrained merrymaking; there was universal teasing, mockery, and clowning. On each of these festivals no work was done; many of the conventions were ignored and acts of license were indulged in. Counterparts of these have occurred in other areas and eras.

New Year's in Rome and in Europe in the Middle Ages—

observed in medieval France as the Feast of Fools—was a day of some revelry and license, and was celebrated with mummery, burlesque, and horseplay. Among many of us New Year's Eve is observed as a carnival occasion for drinking, music, dancing, amatory permissiveness, pranks, noisemaking, and general merriment and boisterousness. April Fools' Day is a time for playing practical jokes or tricks on associates, especially those that make the victims look or act like fools. May Day originally was, and still is in some parts, a day of joy and festival celebrating spring and plant, animal and human increase and fertility, notably with the carrying in procession of green branches or garlands, the setting up of a Maypole and dance about the Maypole. In some parts of medieval Europe it also came to provide an annual moral holiday as youths repaired to the woods for unrestrained lovemaking. Halloween, the evening before All Saints' or All-hallows Day—called Mischief Night in the north of England—is an evening given to masquerading, harmless pranks, and parties for children and young folks. In the United States it has mainly come to be a house-to-house expedition by the children as they demand "trick or treat." In Louisiana, parts of Mississippi and Florida, and some Latin countries Mardi Gras is celebrated, during the three days ending with Shrove Tuesday, with revelry and processions. In some of its manifestations it seems to be a means of building up a sort of reserve or bank or release or license to last through the rigorous restraints of Lent.

Some types of special days have had fun and laughter as a sort of side objective. Historically, market days and fairs with economic exchange and exhibition and sale of produce and products as the main objective have quite generally also offered extra opportunities for diversion, amusement, pleasuring and visiting. In fact, the side shows, an invariable part of fairs, have not been entirely secondary. In most of the types of occasions here mentioned there has been some release of pent-up repression.

Another special example of a formalized means of blowing off steam is the joking relationship among numerous primitive peoples. This has been widely reported by ethnographers as occurring in Africa, Asia, Oceania, and North America, and definitively defined and analyzed by Radcliffe-Brown (90–116). This is a standardized social relationship "between two persons in which one is by custom permitted, and in some instances required, to tease or make fun of the other, who in turn is required to take no offense" (90). It is found particularly in the kinship system where a large number of restraining taboos involving social spacings and avoidances affect the relationship between certain categories of relatives, especially between those who stand in a potential sex relationship, or sometimes between those separated by sharp status differentiations. It often exists in such relationships as those between persons whose fathers belong to the same clan or phratry, between a man and his wife's younger sister or a woman and her husband's younger brother, between cross-cousins of opposite sex, between grandparents and grandchildren.

While there are variations from society to society, in general the respective parties may, without regard for the standard proprieties and with entire impunity, joke together, tease and play practical jokes on each other, exchange abuse and banter, make vulgar or obscene references, even indulge in rather excessive intimacy. The jesting relationship is usually accompanied by loud, specially toned laughter; it is, in fact, a context in which people are able to laugh freely and uproariously about matters and actions otherwise tabooed. It is supposed to make everybody happy.

Of particular point, we have here the very reverse of avoidance relationship. There is not only licensed joking, but especially stylized license with its permitted disrespect and its privileged freedom to ease the rigidity and strain of the "proper" kinship relations.

There are certain benefits over and above the prime ones of easing the relationships between kinsmen with respect to tabooed intimacies of freedom of relationship. Sometimes the joking relationship functions as a way of easing tensions in situations involving status contradictions, thus providing some momentary freedom from the pecking order, and serving as an equalizer. Above all, the playful antagonism discourages friction, hostility, and disjunction, and helps to maintain social unity and peace within the kinship system (which usually is society-wide); it enables the persons and parties to keep conjoined in an alliance by jokes, teasing, and laughter.[5]

Joke-induced laughter is widely resorted to as a means of easing strain in many other forms of relationships between individuals. Its use between competitors and rivals is well known; for example, sales representatives of competing companies joking at luncheon or when they meet on the street; clerks in offices, tellers in banks, sales assistants in retail establishments, using it to avoid clash and strain as they vie with each other for positional favors or sales (Bradney).

C. Choral laughter in a group which is tense due to a consciousness of errors, misdoings, blunders, etcetera, committed by it, not only functions as a defense against a feeling of guilt, but often brings a catharsis of the group concern or discontent with itself and its feeling of guilt. Such laughter frequently seems to arise almost spontaneously. The informal leader or director may seek to develop such laughter to ease a situation.

Related to this is the resort to humor and laughter by outcasts, scalawags, prostitutes, criminals, and other deviates as a way of overcoming a sense of defeat, or of expressing defiance.

D. Laughter may provide subconscious satisfaction when we perceive social lapses of all kinds, including our own spilled milk which cannot be remedied. We can adjust, however, by "laughing it off."

E. Laughter aids in accommodating social requirements to human infirmities, frailties, and idiocies. At the same time that laughter supports the standards and codes, it may also show good-natured tolerance, and a readiness to excuse minor infractions due to human weakness, bumbling, or absentmindedness.

7. SOCIAL PROVISION FOR LICENSED RIDICULE

Societies—primitive, ancient, medieval, modern—have provided, or at least permitted, more or less patterned means of using

---

[5] On the primitive joking relationship see also Montagu, 1967: 11-13; Thomson.

ridicule publicly as a means of releasing pent-up feelings of aggression. Recognizing the dangers of repression and the desirability for publicly expressing disapproval, they have devised instruments and occasions for licensed or institutionalized ridicule of members of the group or collectivity for some acts disapproved in the culture, and also of officials and other prominent or eminent personages. Mocking songs are sung, games played, contests conducted, and special events provided to carry out public ridicule. The annual formal banquet of the Gridiron Club—composed of some fifty top flight Washington newspaper correspondents, with a guest list of prominent government officials and persons of national political importance up to the President himself—is probably the best-know occasion for licensed ridicule in the United States. Songs, skit and dances ridicule and caricature the powerful and the prominent.[6]

8.   TOTALITARIAN LAUGHTER

Irreverent, heretical, and in many instances illicit humor and the accompanying laughter on the part of a suppressed or oppressed people has appeared again and again in history as a means of living with the pressures of extreme control wielded over them by the managers of social power. Such laughter has been used against constituted authorities when in the opinion of the people they exceeded their formally authorized power. It has especially flourished in absolutistic or tyrannical totalitarian systems, including some of a religious kind. Release from tension is one of laughter's most important effects. The principles to be mentioned apply to most situations involving totalitarian regimes.

Two different kinds of relational situations are involved: (*a*) the jokes and other humor devices, and the laughter of the oppressed citizens or subjects *within* the system dominated by the dictator or dictatorial clique, and (*b*) those of the *outside* observers, those in other countries.

---

[6] For historical examples from various cultures and a more extended treatment of licensed ridicule see Elliott, 66-87.

A. Within the totalitarian system the great bulk of the population has had to submit to the system at least overtly, as long as it has retained its vitality. However, there is invariably an undercurrent of restlessness and protest, ready to spring up against the dominators. The dictatorship provides no institutionalized safety valves to release this omnipresent head of steam. To do so would be a confession of weakness. The humorous devices—the clandestine caricature or scrawl on the wall or sidewalk, the anonymously and surreptitiously circulated joke, the stealthy obscenity—and the accompanying veiled and secret joined laughter are resorted to as release mechanisms. Consequently they reflect the spirit of opposition to the absolutistic power of the dictator or other tyrant and he resultant domination and regimentation and cruelty; they express the effort to counteract the fear and the feeling of abasement felt by the citizenry; and they reveal not only de-identification with the dominator but especially the breaking through of the drive for self-assertion. They are often the only means by which the slave-citizen can express his defiance of his drivers (cf. Hanser).

These jokes and other critical devices circulated by the people about their dictators, or told about their own condition in the dictatorship, have several signal utilitarian aspects: (1) they attack (cf. chap. xiii, sec. 2) and usually have some disintegrative effect on the dictator and his regime; (2) they are therapeutic as they ease the hurt of the victims as they are laughingly shared among them; and (3) they are consolidative as they help to unify the sufferers and thus enhance them as a menace to the oppressors. The laughter also produces at least momentary spiritual emancipation.

Psychiatrist William Sargant, on the basis of his observations in two world wars, his experiences with the survivors of concentration camps, and other contacts with such efforts, states that "laughter is the best prophylactic against brainwashing." He discloses that if at any point in the procedure the subjects laugh, "the whole process is wrecked and must be begun all over again." (Cf. Johnson.)

B. The outsiders—other countries or social systems—are often fearsome of the dictatorship as a form of social and political organization, especially during its stage of success and strength, and consider it a threat to their own ideology and operative principles and machinery. They wish to weaken it as much as possible. "Safe" means are eagerly grasped. Thus they relish the contemptuous and derogatory forms of humor that emerge from the dictatorship and fabricate others of their own about it. They abide by Bertolt Brecht's dictum: "One should not fight dictators, one should ridicule them." (Cf. Zijderveld, 287.)

The jokes and other devices, whether from within or without, involve themes related to the pretensions and activities of the dictator or the dictatorial regime. They center on the absurdities, weaknesses, and mistakes which point to the dictator's over-reaching himself through his ignorance or incompetence; they lampoon the self-styled or party-styled savior, or hero, or perfect man, or superman—the all-powerful and all-wise; they throw sharp light on the grotesque realities and patent ludicrous failures of the regime. In general they utilize one of the key laughter situations: the obvious incongruity between the pretentious and grandiose plans and promises on the one hand and the banalities and failures on the other.

These laughter-inducing devices have the advantage of being uncontrollable. Press, radio, television, gatherings of organizations, can be monitored, but satirical and derogatory thrusts as whispered between two or three friends meeting on the street or within the family circle or among passengers in a crowded bus cannot. The secret police and stool pigeons cannot regulate everything the people think or say.

In his excellent article reviewing especially the part of the "political joke" in the dictatorships of the post–World War I period Hanser points out, with numerous examples, that these jokes as found in Germany, Czechoslovakia, Romania, Poland, and the Soviet Union, especially during the 1940's, assumed a significance far beyond their actual content. "They were sub-surface glints of truth that pierced the fog of official propaganda," and the dictators greatly feared the jokes. He refers to Sidney Smith's observation that "there are few who would not rather be hated than laughed at," and himself concludes that the dictators "are content to be hated, but . . . are terrified of laughter, for no one who laughs at them can be wholly deceived, wholly subdued." In such situations laughter makes for freedom.

An obvious converse aspect of laughter in different types of political structures is that critical political humor and laughter flourish best in a democratic society. The tyrant or despot may sometimes make jokes freely and in public about himself or against his subordinates in the regime, but for the public to do so is treason; hence the public laughter against him must be guarded or clandestine. In a democracy, as our own history abundantly demonstrates, both the private and public critics of our public officials, however exalted in position the officials may be, are free to subject them to almost any degree of critical or derogatory humorous thrust without fear of surveillance or punishment. This—and it also applies to our non-political power elite —tends to restrain our power wielders from ever reaching for absolutistic power.

9. LAUGHTER AT THE SCAPEGOAT

A reverse of the laughter of the victims of a totalitarian system as a therapy in their relations with the persecutors is the laughter of the dominant ethnic majority of a nation in crisis situations against the scapegoat minority. People throughout history have employed the scapegoat technique when in a state of turmoil whether economic, social, religious, political, or military. The technique basically consists in using an individual or, in most instances, an alien resident minority group as the object upon which the blame, anger, resentment, and frustration of the majority is saddled for the misfortune they are suffering in a crisis situation. The scapegoat minority usually is conspicuous though socially weak and almost without the power to retaliate. As sacrificial victims the minority members, individually and collectively, are subjected to indecencies and cruelties: derision, invectives, harrassments, assaults, withholding of civil rights, massacres, expulsions, expropriations.

In effect, scapegoating produces satisfactions of escape, defense, and release for its majority perpetrators. The scapegoat
becomes the excuse for their frailties, ineptness, failure, bungling,
indecency. To it they transfer their fears. Incidentally, through
it they exemplify their deep-seated and annoying sense of guilt,
for the scapegoat emphatically states, "J'accuse!" Conspicuous
examples of scapegoats are the Jews, wherever they have so-
journed since the Diaspora. In the United States the Negro has
been the major tragic victim.

Laughter at the scapegoat, though a usual accompaniment,
is a minor and mild part of the victimizing action of the majority,
and a lesser and relatively moderate expression of their hatred.
It does, however, have some therapeutic aspects for them. The
laughter-inducing means are such as macabre and obscene jokes,
caricaturing, resort to vicious but supposedly funny pranks, and
sadistic manhandling. The laughter indulged in by the scape-
goater against the "objectionable" characteristics of the scapegoats is often a substitute for the laughter which he could
rationally and justly direct against himself. By means of it he
attempts to annihilate his own evils.

The herd laughter against the victims also serves to express
triumph over them. In some measure it justifies the treatment of
them. In addition it is a form of draining off the common antipathy and sadistic impulses of the majority against the minority.

10.   AMERICAN NEGRO HUMOR AS SELF
AND GROUP THERAPY

American Negro humor with its related laughter (not typical
of Negroes in general) is a noteworthy instance of laughter as
therapeutic agent in a situation of social tension. It has grown
out of a condition of enforced subordination and separation,
which has created a background of resentment, resistance, and
struggle. Laughter at the contradictions the Negro has found
between his condition and that of most whites, contradictions in
the contentions and the actions of white men, laughter at the
impotence of the "superior" white man in coping with Negro

lies, sabotage, malingering, pretended witlessness has made it possible for him to live with the conditions. Much of the Negro's laughter has been contrived and artificial: a means of placating the white dominators, a psychological weapon of appeasement and appeal. His laughter has offered him protection, consolation, relief, and "often an escape into pride and dignity." As W. E. B. DuBois once wrote, American Negro humor is in part "a defense mechanism," "a reaction from tragedy." "In part it supplies those inner pleasures and gratifications which are denied in broad outline to a caste-ridden and restricted people." In the same vein, James Weldon Johnson has said: "I have learned that this ability to laugh heartily is, in part, the salvation of the American Negro. It has done much to keep him from going the way of the Indian."[7]

As Jerry Buck put it recently, for a hundred years Negro humor has been a convenient foxhole for the Negro to dive into for shelter in time of need. But this has changed very much since the beginning of the civil-rights movement, especially during the last two decades. The American Negro now is on the march and not seeking solace. His humor is increasingly militant, aggressive, accusatory—the humor of Dick Gregory rather than of Stepin Fetchit or Rochester.

The American white's laughter over his own jokes at the Negro's expense has been in part a release from the guilt felt by a troubled person, as Myrdal (38-39) has said: "When people are up against great inconsistencies in their creed and behavior which they cannot, or do not want to account for rationally, humor is the way out. It gives a symbolic excuse for imperfections, a point to what would otherwise be ambiguous."

11. POLITICAL HUMOR AS THERAPEUTIC STRATEGY

Humor and laughter have been and still are used by American political figures. Some have found that a humorous attitude

---

[7] Both quotations are given without source in the excellent study by Sterling, esp. 21-25.

toward their job has been a great aid in enabling them to live with its toils and distractions and disappointments. Dean Acheson declared, after his turbulent years as Secretary of State, that "public men should take their jobs seriously—but not themselves."

Public figures, of course, are constant and perennial targets of our professional humorists, who seek to put the ideas and ways of their subjects in a critical (predominantly) or approving light. What is of special note here is that some of the public, especially the political figures, use laughter in their own behalf. They ingratiate themselves with the public with their sense of humor and their ability to chuckle at their own absurdities. They frequently seek to attract laughter to and at themselves as a means of detracting attention or deflecting the effects of their fumbling or bumbling.

Many a public figure has aided his cause by telling good stories on himself. Early in the present century William Howard Taft delighted his audiences by calling himself "the worst licked man who ever ran for President"; and William Jennings Bryan never failed to win a response by referring back to 1896 when he "first began running for the Presidency."

Humor, while usually used to some extent in political campaigns (Harris), was especially resorted to during the summer of 1968 by those trying to get to the White House. Much of it was self-deprecatory, as they joked merrily about their own shortcomings and failures, thus inviting a good-natured, good-sport, and sympathetic response from the electorate. Some of it also—as in the past—consisted of not so sly humorous digs at the characteristics, or well-known typical behaviors, or prevailing images of opponents in the race.

The present chapter has been largely devoted to a discussion of the sociologically pertinent aspects of suppressive laughter in society, though aggressive laughter has also been touched upon. It is quite likely that as long as there is social suppression, there will be suppressive laughter. At any rate, it seems that when suppression disappears in an area of social relationships, then repressive laughter vanishes. By way of summary, it can be indicated that laughter has important psychiatric qualities and has great value in maintaining both individual and group mental health. Its capabilities as a therapeutic agent of great versatility are manifold. Rapp (1951: 173) concludes: "Laughter and the sense of humor are among man's greatest blessings; they constitute an extraordinarily effective aid to physical and mental health. In the many woes which never happen; in the thousand and one strains and stresses and pressures of modern living; in the annoyances, disappointments, failures, and frustrations; a moment of 'time out' for hearty laughter will help throw off the poisons which might accumulate in our bodies and minds and it will help us prepare for fresh activity."[8]

---

[8] On laughter in general as release, and especially suppressive laughter, see Rapp, 1947: 209; 1949: 93-96; 1951: 109-113, 120, 167-173.

XIII. The Hostile Uses of Laughter

Brief mention has been made of the nature of aggressive or hostile laughter (chap. iv), and its relation to group maintenance (chap. viii), social control (chap. ix), conduct of status relations (chap. xi), and its therapeutic functions for groups (chap. xii). Here we present some basic principles regarding its place as a form of social behavior, some reasons for its prevalence, and especially some of the more important uses of it in social and societal relations.

Hostile laughter is the laughter widely employed in laughing at or against others. It is to be contrasted with comic laughter, the laughter of amusement, and happy or joyous laughter. It is a form of behavior quite to be expected. Aggression is a common propulsive behavioral feature, and most people seek outlets for their aggressive urges. Many interactions are competitive. Social life is full of hostility. Individuals and groups attempt to assert themselves over others, dominate others, successfully oppose others. Thus it is understandable that much of our fun-making consists in deriding or taking a crack at someone. In fact, a contest, whether waged with sticks and stones or with thrusts or gusts of hostile laughter, is the liveliest kind of fun. But hostile laughter goes far beyond making fun of others. Among children coming home from school rough-housing and outlaughing one another seem to go together. The commonest of all jokes are the ones whose point lies in the downing or degradation or incapacitation of a rival or potential rival.

This discussion leads us to the extreme negative pole of the continuum of societal effects, functions, and uses of laughter indicated in the treatment of it as a societal agent (chap. vii, sec. 2). Hostile laughter is the laughter of opposition and antagonism. It is used to victimize, attack, harm, or defeat some person or group. We will treat it from the point of view of two main and closely related negative uses: (1) as a rejective, separative, and excluding technique, and (2) as a mechanism for punishing and carrying on conflict against other persons or collectivities.

1.   THE REJECTIVE AND EXCLUDING EFFECT AND USE OF LAUGHTER

Being laughed at as individual or collectivity by another individual or collectivity is generally accepted as not only a means of criticism, derision, or ridicule; it may also be a means of rejection and exclusion, and can effect separation, isolation, and segregation.

When one part of a collectivity laughs derisively at another part, or when one of two heretofore closely related collectivities laughs at the other, the effect is to bring about secession; indeed, it may be done intentionally to produce this very result.

Joined laughter within a group or collectivity, whether spontaneous or deliberately purposive, separates the combination of joined laughers from all non-participants and frequently is a means of excluding the outsiders, the foreigners, those unwanted by the group or collectivity. We have already noted that many laughter themes are confined to particular culture groups and areas, and hence, that boundaries exist between collectivities on the basis of what the people laugh about and at. That laughing together at others may reflect dislike of them or disunity with them has also been briefly treated. Here we stress that joined laughter can also be a repellent or barrier against others. The clique, whether of children or adults, bars the non-clique persons by jointly laughing at them; hardheaded businessmen use similar risible tactics to keep away from the idealistic eggheads; the sexes laugh at each other to prevent the intrusion of one into the closed order of the other; those socially in, by laughing at all the hoi polloi, protect (and possibly excuse) themselves from free association with them.

Hostile laughter is used by persons or collectivities to keep out disapproved beliefs, ideas, forms of speech, habits, social manners, and forms of dress. Lumley (276–277) referred to such laughter as "a prophylactic against contamination."

A rarely recognized aspect of laughter used with hostile intent is not its exercise but the deliberate withholding of it or the refusal to acknowledge it as an act of expression of attitude, or of communication, or as an influence in social control. Laughter as a social act, whether friendly or hostile, whether with or at or against others, whether purposive or non-purposive, implies some reciprocity, some giving and receiving, between the laughter stimulator or elicitor and the recipient or target of the stimulating or eliciting effort. Some forms of impairment of this reciprocity—those forms deliberately engaged in—can have socially significant hostile effect. Thus the intentional avoidance of or refusal to extend the laugh or smile or chuckle of greeting or friendliness when confronted with acquaintances is often resorted to as a studied expression of disapproval or an act of insult or denigration. Conversely, the refusal of the intended target to recognize the antagonistic laugh of the attacking opponent can neutralize its hostile effect. Such laughter behaviors are means of cutting or refusing to identify with another person or persons, or of bringing them to heel. They are brutal but also often effective rejective or punitive techniques.[1]

---

[1] Note, however, that not all impairment of reciprocity in laughter or lack of response to inducements or invitations to exchange of laughter is due to deliberate hostile intent of one or more of the parties in the contact situation. The following alternative sociocultural factors can be inferred from chap. v, secs. 1-4, and chap. vi, sec. 3: (*a*) There are some people almost without any sense of humor at any time. They do not respond to the humorist, nor do they recognize a situation as humorous, simply because they are immune, or dead, to humor. (*b*) The humor involved may be too subtle for, or beyond, the target person or group. This may be due to an intelligence gap between the respective parties. (*c*) The participants—humorist and target—because of an educational or cultural sophistication gap, may live in such different cultural worlds that there is no exchange of meanings. In both *b* and *c* the humorist's sally goes right past the target.

2. LAUGHTER AS A CONFLICT TECHNIQUE

Aggressive, sardonic, satirical, or otherwise hostile laughter is also a mechanism widely and purposively resorted to in order to oppose other persons, or the behaviors of other persons or groups. In its most extreme social uses it goes further than merely attempting to warn, or correct, or control, or exclude others. It is used as a means of carrying on conflict, as a weapon for attacking, thwarting and hurting those against whom it is directed individually or collectively. This is laughter *against* other individuals, or groups, or factions or organizations. The conflict thus carried on, like conflict in general, is a fight for power, for dominance, for supremacy, for conquest, for the ability to determine policy, or to achieve freedom from control, or to protect and fulfill ideas, beliefs, ways, goals. Defeat of the target is sought. Such laughter may be highly effective. Men have long known that if they can make any man or group or concept or belief or social movement an object of derisive laughter, he or it is weakened and possibly doomed to failure.

The conflict is waged with varying degrees of intensity and severity. The laughers may seek to humiliate or malign the opponents, to weaken or injure them, to coerce them, to punish them, to eliminate them from the scene, and in the extreme to annihilate them so far as their participation in the particular type or instance of situation is concerned. The laughter itself may range from mild to violent.

We make fun of those with whom we are rivals; we even rig situations in order to bring malicious laughter down on competitors or people we do not like and thus humble them. As groups or organizations or nations we use the laughter of mockery, contempt, derision and ridicule, and the specific tools of malign jokes, invective, caricature, satirical pieces, hostile repartees, and comic obscenities against the enemy to undermine his morale and undercut his reputation, strength, and position.

Two tools for waging opposition by means of wit deserve special mention. Satire has been discussed both generally and as a tool in social control (chap. ix, sec. 2). It also is a widely resorted to means of directing hostile laughter against persons, groups, organizations, institutions, attitudes, proposals, ideologies, and so on, that are opposed by some element of the population. As noted earlier, satire can turn the spotlight on the enemies and evils of society and function as a potent instrument of criticism and censure. But it can go beyond these, and function as a more or less jocular but pointed way of worsting an opponent. What is more, it is used as a technique for attacking or eliminating the absurd, the ridiculous, the perverse, the outrageous, the evil of persons, groups, and institutions. Satire as a tool for conflict runs from bitter invective through harsh derision, ridicule, banter, and sarcasm[2] to the most delicate irony. It brings out weaknesses or perversities by exaggerating them or by obviously diminishing or demeaning them. It is largely a device by and for the more intelligent because its effectiveness rests on logical ability, the ability to detect overstatement or understatement, or the subtly incredible.

Hostile repartee is a highly sophisticated form of conflict, It is a kind of person-versus-person encounter—a contest in expression—that usually seeks laughter as an end. It is a duel of wits between two clever face-to-face antagonists in some competitive situation involving smart verbal attack and sharp enjoinder. As Eastman put it (1936: 227-230), "It is word play taking the place of sword play. It is a duel fought with the points of jokes." According to Rapp (1951: 92, 103-108), it "is striking back in revenge for being struck." The purpose is to take down the opponent, to put him in a bad light, to damage him by means of a damning retort. It is usually a deliberate playing to the gallery; the audience just sits back and laughs over each *touché* (Rapp, 1951: 104).

Here is a classic vitriolic gem—

Gladstone (to Disraeli after one of their violent arguments): "Sir, you will end either upon the gallows or of a venereal disease."

---

[2] *Sarcasm* is derived from the Greek word that means "flesh-tearing."

"I suppose that depends," said Disraeli, "upon whether I embrace your principles or your mistress."[3]

Rapp comments (1951: 105): "That's about as playful as a cobra that's been poked by a stick." Such repartee is savage and cruel, and yet it is laugh-provoking. You first gasp, and then laugh when you have recovered from the viciousness of the rapier thrust.

Laughter is used as a weapon of opposition to superiors, to oppressors, to those wielding power and authority, with special reference to dictators and tyrants. The political joke has been a device widely used in the countries ridden by totalitarian regimes by the slave-citizens to attack their absolutistic oppressors (cf. chap. xii, sec. 9). It has also been a favorite implement of non-totalitarian societies as they have waged ideological war against the dictatorial regimes and their principles. The following (quoted by Hanser, 13) is an example, circulated in Poland.

> Little Ladislaw was called upon to recite for the benefit of a Communist official checking up on education under the Polish People's Republic.
>
> "Who is your father?" the teacher asked.
>
> "Stalin," said Ladislaw promptly, "the father of all progress."
>
> "Very good," said teacher. "And who is your mother?"
>
> "The Soviet Union, mother of all peace-loving people."
>
> "Excellent!" the official broke in. "And now tell me, my little man, what would you like to be when you grow up?"
>
> "An orphan," replied little Ladislaw.

Hostile laughter may be resorted to by individuals and groups to subtly negate the intended efforts of more or less aggressive movements to influence or persuade them. For example, many people laugh derogatorily or with sardonic amusement—"give the

---

[3] An earlier version goes back some 200 years. In the House of Commons the Earl of Sandwich, himself a notorious ladies' man, roared at the libertine and libertarian John Wilkes: "I am convinced, Mr. Wilkes, that you will die either of pox or on the gallows." Wilkes parried: "That, my lord, depends on whether I embrace your mistress or your principles." (*Time*, Nov. 8, 1968, p. 32.)

merry ha-ha"—to many noisy (blatant) or overdone, or otherwise offensive radio and television advertisements and thus defeat the intended effect.

In the international area hostile governments utilize laughter for attack. Through their foreign intelligence services (our CIA, e.g.) they spread about seemingly flippant but actually carefully devised witticisms, especially jests and jokes, to lampoon and demean, sometimes to expose, key personages and crucial activities of opposing countries. It is a useful tactic in psychological warfare.

Hostile laughter is often both an economical social agent and one capable of rather subtle use. It is the transference to a less active plane of the overt action involved in conducting a thrashing.[4] It has the advantage of permitting us to make our enemy appear ridiculous or to confound his strategy without resort to outright verbal or physical attack. It can also be shrewdly used to exercise aggression or malice in situations where the actors are unable to engage in these openly and directly because of laws, moral codes, or conventions, as in attacking marriage or the church. Hostile wit, in fact, is often a sly and relatively safe way of engaging in slanderous, even libelous, activity.

An often overlooked use of aggressive laughter relates to the ancient principle that the best defense is often a good attack. To launch a good counterlaugh against your assailants—those individuals or groups or organizations trying to harm you, propagandize you, take you in—is to forestall or block or neutralize their attack.

Another countereffect of hostile laughter, from the point of view of strategy, is that when laughter is used for attack it may function as an irritant or a goad to those laughed at, and induce a backlash of retaliatory or punitive tactics, and possibly accelerate the hostility. Some malicious laughter is obviously sadistic.

Even among the well-bred, if the attack on the opponent has been more or less successful, it may be celebrated by the cutting stentorian laughter of triumph or conquest.

---

[4] On conflict functions of humor and laughter see Stephenson.

XIV. Laughter and Socialization

This discussion of laughter as a socializing influence and agent epitomizes the treatment of the sociocultural and societal effects, functions and uses of laughter as it brings out especially the potency and versatility of laughter as a force in this basic social process. It also indicates that laughter is a largely undiscovered and unrecognized factor in socialization and that it plays a much greater part than is ordinarily realized.

1. A SUPPLEMENTARY AGENT IN INFORMAL SOCIALIZATION

Laughter, of course, is only one of a complex of factors in socialization. It is an informal supplementary agent—supplementary to, and, in the main, reinforcing the institutionally organized agents. It has certain peculiar and unique functions and effects. It can subtly penetrate sectors and corners of social life that the more formalized and highly institutionalized agents cannot. It is also a sort of bonus assist in socialization in that it provides or incites to much spontaneous and continuous informal socialization. Its functioning mainly in an informal and unorganized manner means that it has a lower level of conspicuousness as agent and hence is largely overlooked as a factor in socialization.

2. THE NATURE OF SOCIALIZATION

Socialization itself is the congeries of processes and procedures whereby the inhabitants of a societal area are subjected, continuously and persistently, to a host of sociocultural influences, pressures, and controls, which pervasively surround them like an atmosphere, and develop them throughout their lives into tolerable associates and participants. Socialization, in general, is a conditioning, inducting, instructing, training, disciplining, correcting, motivating, sanctioning, and absorbing process operating among the interacting individuals and groups. Its over-all function is to produce socii fitted for life in an orderly, organized, purposive, and functionally efficient society. It comes about as a concomitant of the individual's lifelong participation in the ongoing sociocultural life of his society. More specifically, it is the over-all process by which the values, attitudes, norms, roles, skills, objectives, definitions, and rationalizations of orderly and effective social living of a given community or society are so ingrained in the personality of the individuals that their behavior is largely in conformity with the norms and ends. The socialized person conforms generally in his likes and dislikes, his aspirations, and his actions to the requirements of his social systems.

3.   WHAT LAUGHTER DOES AS SOCIALIZING AGENT

A.   It should be realized at the outset that laughter in some form is potentially present in almost every interaction of two or more persons, and since every interact has some socializing affect, that laughter is universal, time-tested, and omnipresent. Individuals and groups cannot avoid being subjected to laughter as a socializing influence and agent; they cannot escape from it.

B.   Communication is elemental in socialization. Laughter, as has been noted repeatedly, is non-symbolic communication. It functions as an effective means of transmitting many of the essentials of socialization among the interacting persons, groups, and categories. Correlatively, an important aspect of socialization of and for the individual is for him to learn the language of laughter, particularly the meanings that laughter communicates when it is directed *at* him.

negative, whether spontaneous or consciously purposive, whether

C.   The laughter of associates, whether socially positive or acting directly or indirectly, whether unifying and equalizing or separative, rejective, or antagonistic, is a socializing factor in the life of every individual from babyhood on. It operates as such in many types of social situations as it provides various behavioral cues in these situations. Its main structural settings are the family, especially for children as they are affected by the accepting, approving, and disapproving laughter of both parents and siblings, the peer groups, and the organizations which they are a part of or which function for them as reference groups.

D. Some of the outstanding features of laughter are epitomized as it functions in the socialization of the child. This involves the laughter at and with the child by his elders, both within and outside the family, and his peers or associates. Through the laughter of associates, both elders and peers, the child learns a great many things that count in his socialization:

1) By being laughed at and by laughing with others he develops a consciousness of himself vis-à-vis others.

2) He learns about social authority as it resides in parents and other elders, siblings, and peers, whose laughter means most in the exercise of and submission to authority.

3) He learns about social coercion and exclusion under the oppression of disapproving laughter.

4) The laughter helps focus his attention on important social facts such as (*a*) many of society's basic operational principles, ethical principles, standards and codes, (including etiquette forms); (*b*) important social taboos; (*c*) approval-winning behavior and the relation of this to social codes; (*d*) the costs to himself of violation of standards and rules, including the momentary children's conventions; (*e*) the actions that invite retaliation; (*f*) the nature and content "desirables"; (*g*) the meanings and names of many things for which he is laughed at because of his lack of knowledge about them or for his mistakes.

Most of these effects of laughter, of course, also apply to adults, but they are especially pertinent in childhood.

E. There are wider implications of laughter as lifelong socializer of human beings:

1) It inculcates an awareness of, and emphatically affirms and promotes, the common values and norms.

2) It teaches the essentials of the social system's roles and statuses, underscores the behavioral patterns necesary for the performance of the roles, and those necessary to the individual in occupying the particular statuses that his societal life requires or permits him to assume.

3) It signals deficient or aberrant conduct, disapproves of incorrect behavior, and more or less forcefully suggests caution and correction if punishment is to be avoided—thus pointing to standards of excellence, and potentially reinforcing correct behavior.

4) It sensitizes individuals, groups, and other population segments to the dominant judgments and expectations of groups or society.

5) Like most socialization agents it provides sanctions. The joys of laughing with others, or of receiving approving laughter from others, serves as a reward. It also helps to motivate individuals and groups to behave in socially approved and socially expected ways. Critical or ridiculing laughter at or against the individual is usually keenly felt as punishment.

F. The experience with laughter, especially with being laughed at, is often remembered, sometimes poignantly, by the individuals affected by it. These memories tend to create a bank, or store, of precaution against involvement in desocializing activity. Thus past as well as present laughter is effective; and fear of critical, antagonistic, or punitive laughter safeguards the future behavior of individuals. As a result it is possible that persons are so innerly conditioned and developed that they act almost automatically in regularized fashion, not only unconsciously and automatically but willingly and from conviction bred of experience.

G. Laughter is also important in the repeated resocialization of the individual. For example, when new statuses and roles are assumed, as in the case of the newly married or the new incumbents of a job, or when newcomers are in the process of assimilation in a new community or society, the individuals try to avoid being laughed at because of their ignorance or clumsiness. In general, as laughter criticizes and ridicules ineptness and archaisms in the behavior of the individual and shakes him out of bad habits, outmoded attitudes, obsolescent roles and inexperience, on the one hand, and as it approves and encourages newly acquired knowledge, newly demonstrated skills, newly learned and practiced etiquette forms, on the other, it promotes adjustment to the changing forces and the new institutional exigencies and necessities of the individuals and groups. The underlying principle, of course, grows from the laughter's continually reflecting place and time. It thus confronts the people with the ever-changing and new situations. It teaches them new facts, provides new awarenesses, makes new demands, presses new disciplines upon them.

4. RELATION OF LAUGHING ASSOCIATES TO THE INDIVIDUAL

Not all associates are equally significant or equally effective as critical or sustaining laughers. Correlatively, the individual has differential susceptibility to those laughing with or at him. In his instruction, correction, and motivation he is much more affected by the laughter of some people than of others. The amount and kind of socializing effect depends on whether the target is socially and psychologically aware of those laughing at or against him, is sensitive to them by virtue of the respective social positions, and perceives the meaning and intent of their laughter.

A. The basic principle is that socialization takes place primarily through social interaction with people who are significant others for him. The laughter of the people who matter most has the most social control effect. If the persons are not important to him, he may ignore their laughter or easily brush it off.

1) The laughter with people with whom the individual has frequent contact is more effective in most instances than that of those with whom he has only occasional or no contacts.

2) The laughter of strangers is less important, significant, and determinative than that of the people he knows and is involved with.

3) Similarly, the laughter of those with whom the individual agrees is more important for him than that of those with whom he disagrees. It is possible that if the target violently disagrees with the laughers, for example, because they support a different set of values, he may consider their laughing *at* him a compliment.

4) The other laughers diminish in importance to the individual as their social distance from him increases. Those way out on the periphery do not matter at all; the laughter of peers or equals has marked effect.

5) Especially significant is the laughter of (*a*) the members of the reference groups which are more or less determinative in the values, choices, and acts of the individual; (*b*) people of higher social position and of prestige; (*c*) people who exercise authority over the individual, or have some control over the rewards and punishments of the individual: (*d*) people who are members of groups (especially organizations) that the individual is trying to imitate or emulate or join.

For the target in all of these situations or circumstances, the critical or antagonistic laughter hurts him; approving laughter reassures and sustains him.

In general, the individual's own appraisal of the particular situation, his own estimate of his own position relative to others, his social evaluation of those laughing at him, and his personal aspirations in the situation affect his reactions.

B. There may be a considerable variation in the categories of significant others in the course of the life cycle of the individual. In the earlier life stages the approving or critical-corrective laughter of parents, siblings (the small boy and his highly regarded older brother), close playmates, or other heroes are likely to be highly important. Later in life, it is the upper level members of hierarchical organizations of which he is a part, or groups or categories of individuals he is anxious to enter.

XV. The Social Control
of Laughter

The present chapter briefly indicates some of the social hazards that inhere in laughter in social life both because of certain of its intrinsic characteristics and its exercise and use by individuals and groups deficient in social sensitivity, decency, wisdom and humanity. It especially points to certain cautions, limitations, and controls devised and utilized to reduce its misuse, and to taboos placed on certain of its uses by individuals or groups that fear it or wish to manipulate it in their own behalf.

1. LAWLESS OR ANARCHIC LAUGHTER

Laughter in some of its major and typical expressional forms is associated with the upsetting or violation of normal, customary, conventional, or otherwise established patterns of social action. Such laughter gains its impulse and zest from departures from fixed norms, attitudes, beliefs, and preconceived ideas of the way things should be. It implies at least momentary freedom or even secession from the dictates of particular moral, religious, aesthetic, or other valued social codes. In sum, such laughter provides a holiday from social control. Potentially this lawlessness or anarchy can impose serious social strains and cause weaknesses in societal operation.

2. SOCIALLY UNDESIRABLE LAUGHTER

Laughter can be a powerful agent for social ill. When unchecked it can take on ugly and pernicious forms. It can easily be deliberately stimulated and manipulated by unscrupulous persons or groups for anti-social ends, thus making for indecency, cruelty, or stupid, reckless, or irresponsible usage. In its public forms it can defeat worthy persons and causes, and it can be a mighty instrument of group tyranny. Even as it produces conformity, some of the conformity may be of no benefit to the group, but costly to the individual laughed at. Like all instruments it can be overused. Thus societies and their sub-elements, in order to keep laughter in some of its guises and forms from getting out of hand, quite generally impose some limits and restraints upon it. (Sully, 418-422; Armstrong, 59.)

3. RESTRAINTS ON THE USE OF LAUGHTER

Different laughters are subjected to different degrees of mainly conventionalized but non-legal controls.[1] We taboo laughter beyond a certain point with respect to many common laughter-eliciting conditions. We can laugh at mild indecencies but not at egregious ones; at small misfortunes (a minor mishap to one's clothing, or chasing a wind-blown hat) but not at major mishaps (a family tragedy); at moderate insults but not at vicious ones; at small misdemeanors but not at felonies.

Several admonitory principles regarding the use of laughter stand out, as do certain unwritten rules and common informal restraints and regulatory principles affecting its interpersonal expression under particular circumstances.

A. Laughter should be used with moderation and circumspection. If unbridled, laughter fails in some of its finest functions—unification, the exercise of discrimination or acumen, and criticism. Attention wavers if laughter is too long continued or too often resorted to. It reaches a point of diminishing returns, occasionally a point of no return. In general, humor loses much of its strength with repetition, as in repeating the same joke or telling a series of jokes that are similar in nature or telling too many at a time. It has been well said (Armstrong, 61): "Men

---

[1] So far as I know there are no legal restrictions on malicious action by laughter similar to those on slander and libel by verbal means.

who are always laughing and who laugh at everything reduce life to a deadly monotony without contrast and without flavor."

Certain sociopsychological awarenesses lead to informal restraint. When critical or derisive laughter is used against others, people of even moderate social wisdom realize that if they go too far—laugh too long or too much or too scornfully or brutally— they arouse hostility in those they seek to correct or censure, as well as in neutral onlookers. This negates the effort. Unreasonable or unbridled laughter may produce alienation and hatred instead of benefiting the targets, and it may endanger the social system. Furthermore, overly vicious or overly bitter accusatory or antagonistic humor and laughter may provoke pity or sympathy for the victim in the observers; and it may lead to a suspicion of the honesty or verity of the motives of the laughers on the part of the observers. A certain amount of humor or witty nonsense, or insulting or malicious laughter can be indulged in without inducing much negative effect; but a point is reached where the flood of silliness or of ill-natured or unseemly laughter bores or nauseates or painfully shocks the audience and quite possibly induces a backlash of open enmity.

B. Because it is so potent, laughter should be used with caution, discretion, tolerance, and charity. The laughter of ridicule, for example, can be a dangerous abusive instrument which wounds deeply. Much of it is therefore toned down in the interest of decency, but the savage element is apt to lurk. When used against an innocent or socially unsophisticated individual or collective victim, it is an act of cruelty and may inflict infinite and permanent damage. People of understanding and goodwill and decency avoid causing personal injury to others by means of laughter. Laughter without observable meaning, regardless of situation or motive, is also usually offensive to people of good sense and good taste. This is implied in the Moroccan proverb: "Laughing without reason comes from lack of good manners."

C. Because laughter underscores and dramatizes social themes, and because it may affect delicate personal relations involving powerful emotions or deeply felt moral and religious considerations, most groups and societies place some informal limits upon laughter under their contemporary customs, conventions, mores, and proprieties. They maintain a sort of floor of decency, morality, humanity, and appropriateness. Most people feel that laughter should be reasonable and just. Hence they especially indicate—though the guidelines are often rather indistinct and fluctuating—what can be safely, decently, and beneficially laughed at, and what cannot. Laughter itself, therefore, is regulated to some extent.

1) Almost all groups have things, types of persons, subjects, and conditions that are too sacred on the one hand, or to blasphemous or too obscene or otherwise too unfitting or indecent on the other, to joke or laugh about publicly. Among us, eschewed or tabooed as objects of laughter are many physical deformities and disabilities, such as those of hunchbacks, paraplegics, cripples, and victims of cerebral hemorrhage and blindness, though some of these have been deemed funny by other cultures. The same is true of excrementary acts. It is also indecent to laugh about some diseased conditions, such as cancer, leprosy, venereal diseases. On the other hand, we laugh at both fatness and skinniness, and have many jokes about deafness, stuttering, and baldness. Today most of our public humorists—especially cartoonists, comic-strip artists, and jokesmiths—avoid barnyard humor, sex, religion, war and mass slaughter, social and economic problem situations such as poverty, unemployment, broken homes, divorce, and increasingly race, nationality, and ethnicity.

The joker is on especially shaky ground in the field of religion. His audience may present a variety of values and convictions regarding the sacred in general, and, in particular, attitudes toward Deity, or theological fundamentals, or organizational ideology, or saints, or clergy, or sanctity and validity of their religious forms and organization, or the incumbents of the various levels of their organizational hierarchy or sacred things. The supernatural is too awesome to lend itself readily or safely to levity. A humorous position which in the opinion of the audience constitutes disrespect to these viewpoints is considered to be an indecorous affront.

Breed (115), some years ago, referred to a study of joking and laughter among Spanish Americans of the Southwest. Strong inhibitions were found against jokes about certain subjects. These included religion, Hispanidad (glorification of the Spanish tradition), and father and father-in-law (the kinship pattern being patriarchal). In religion jokes were permitted about certain themes, such as religious duties and the saints, but no joking was found about core areas, such as the Eucharist, Good Friday, and the Penitente movement.

The underlying principle with respect to the sacred or functionally necessary things seems to be that they are essential to survival and cultural integrity, and expressive of group solidarity; or they have crucial supernatural religious significance. Therefore people cannot afford to lampoon, or degrade, or desanctify them with derisive laughter. Most groups, especially, feel the need of controlling obscenities in at least some elements of the population, notably the young. Tabooing laughter about obscene things and affairs is a way of playing them down and avoiding their ill effects: many people feel restrained about laughing freely and publicly at them.

It has also been touched upon that in status relations it is inadvisable for lower-status persons or levels to laugh at those of a higher bracket, at least in their presence, especially in hierarchical organizations.

2) There are limits—sensed and observed by most of us—to the extent that we may laugh even in fun with good-natured badinage (using banter, quips, and gags) at our acquaintances, our friends, even our spouses, before giving offense. There are also distinct limits to how far we can go before our laughter hurts others (and perhaps ourselves through backlash) in religion and politics and ethnic relations.

Joking has rules of its own. One has no right to play the joking game unless one is willing to take one's turn at being "it." And being it teaches the limits beyond which joking stops being pleasant and becomes annoying or persecutory. Furthermore, any member of a group who goes too far in his joking at others, who fails to observe the unwritten code, cuts himself off from the general sympathy and acceptance of his fellows. (Cf. Seward, 58.)

3) Certain principles seem to govern who can laugh at whom critically in certain types of relationships and group situations. There is, for example, a selective use of laughter in given groups, or group situations, in which carping laughter is safe or deemed permissible for insiders, but is tabooed for outsiders as indecent. The inside joke or the in-group joke is germane here; the members of the in group may use inside jokes against each other, but it is very dangerous for outsiders to use them. Thus a Jew may needle another Jew about his Jewishness, but the non-Jew many not. A Negro may kid another Negro about segregation, but a white man may not. (Cameron, 84.) On the other hand, the outsider can say funny or cutting things about the established institutions of a community or nation that insiders cannot, and get away with it.

4) Certain special occasions, with their particular nature and typical functions have their appropriate humor and laughter; but it is out of place at other occasions and places. For example, laughter is appropriate at cocktail parties, when viewing movie or TV comedies, at night clubs, or at informal gatherings of close associates; but it is proscribed as unseemly on sacred or solemn occasions (for example, funerals), in times of grief or misfortune, in churches, at shrines, or other sacred places, at various familial, political, or religious ceremonies, and other formal occasions. (Cf. also chap. v, sec. 3.)[2]

D. Note also social differentials in laughter control. Different groups and collectivities, depending on the criteria of decency of their subculture, have not only some very different, acceptable laughter themes, but also different laughter taboos. The lower classes of a society can safely laugh at things, or situations, or relations, or occurrences at certain types of occasions that would

---

[2] Certain themes are not touched upon or are deliberately avoided by all except their own most specialized adherents, not because the themes are too sensitive socially, morally, or religiously, but because most people do not know enough about them to see their humorous elements or aspects. This holds particularly in science, literature, and the fine arts.

bring shame and obloquy upon members of the upper classes. The different ethnic groups as compared with each other have different proscriptions regarding the laughable.

4. ATTEMPTS TO CONTROL PUBLIC LAUGHTER

A quite different aspect of the social control of laughter is concerned with efforts to control it by those seeking defense against it or attempting to prevent it on the one hand, and by those with special selfish manipulative, even exploitive, objectives on the other.

These objectives point to a basic aspect of humor and its related laughter as these are socially applied: the interrelation of humor and freedom, and in turn the attitudes and tactics of the wielders of social power as they are confronted with free public laughter.

Inherently, humor, as we have noted, is sportive and spontaneous in contrast to solemn and rigid. It is emancipatory instead of binding. It resists frustration, domination, regimentation, submission, by making these appear ludicrous. In its public forms humor devotes itself to criticism of existing organizations, institutions, beliefs and functionaries as these impinge on the fundamental freedoms of men. The laughter that correlates with, underscores, and expresses this criticism gives freedom and operates as a form of guilt-free aggression against the freedom-thwarting conditions or human agents.

Various persons, social cliques, ethnic elements, authorities, institutional or corporate groups and organizations, and special power segments of the population seek to limit, restrain, deflect, avoid, suppress or abolish that laughter which is directed against them. They do this because they resent or fear the spotlighting, the criticism of, or attack upon their ideas, or actions, or characteristics by free laughter. They view the critical humorous attitudes and the attendant laughter as signs of disrespect, irreverence, subversion, hostility, and in some instances conspiracy, and as threats to the maintenance of their influence, or authority, or power. As Muggeridge (59) has put the matter: "When the governed laugh, the governors cannot but have an uneasy feeling that they may be laughing at them."

Some of the efforts consist in manipulating the contextual situation, especially the laughter-producing personnel and the management of the media organizations. In other instances the would-be controllers seek to gain for their purposes laughter of approval, or of ready acceptance of their aims, or things, or actions, or products.

Laughter control is obvious in many social situations. Historically it has characterized almost all social-status and power-authority systems. The upper social classes and castes and kings and queens have attempted to squelch critical or ridiculing laughter. Today, as in the past, the abolition of humor is virtually pursued in tyrannical and totalitarian societies, and in the main, as Muggeridge (59) states, it "only exists as a kind of Maquis or resistance movement." Laughter at the dictatorial rulers is punishable as a criminal offense. To the extent that public humor is permitted—for example, in the Soviet "humor" journal *Krokodil*—it is pretty innocuous, well-filtered, and painfully unfunny stuff.

Control attitudes and tactics also prevail between the different levels of functionaries of large-scale social organizations, whether economic, political, military, or religious.

Even the members of the power elite in our democratic American communities like to feel free to laugh at the less powerful, and do so condescendingly, but resent and decry humor directed against themselves, and may at least try to informally punish those who show amusement about them and their antics.

Aside from occasional exceptions, in democracies we cannot use laws, or police, or secret service as controlling and punitive devices or agencies; but we can and do use such techniques against the deviant or subversive laughers as the snub, the insult, conspicuous avoidance, and the withholding of preferences, legitimate rewards, promotions, and recognitions.

As a special manipulative tactic we have advertisers in printed media seeking to control the laughter-inducing devices appearing in them. Corporations, in buying magazine advertising space, may bring pressure on the publishers to have cartoons on the same or adjoining page strengthen rather than lampoon or denigrate the subject (e.g., the product) and intent of their advertisement (Beatty).

It is noteworthy that a people's freedom to laugh—freedom to laugh freely, openly and critically at its institutions, beliefs, authorities, diverse ethnic elements, higher status population elements, and so on—indicates a fine state of social, political, economic, and religious freedom in the society or nation.

XVI. Sociolinguistic Aspects of Humor and Laughter

The nascent social subscience of sociolinguistics is revealing new dimensions and vistas of language in the operation of human society. It involves the relationship between language as a crucial factor in social behavior, and in turn the influence of human society on the structure, functions and uses of language. The sociolinguistic approach indicates close reciprocal relations between humor and laughter and language. To be sure, some linguists have been aware of some of these relations, especially of language forms that evoke laughter; but their treatments have usually been colored by their specialized slants as linguists and have been somewhat deficient in the social and cultural orientation of the forms examined.

Two socially significant aspects of language as a form and technique of expression and an instrument of communication are of basic significance in the present analysis and are developed below.

1. THE EFFECT OF THE LANGUAGE SYSTEM ON HUMOR AND LAUGHTER

The language system of a people to a considerable extent determines and limits their humor and their various forms and subjects of laughter. This is because, first, everyone in the society is a member of a language community, and much of what he communicates is by means of the structures of the language; and second, the language itself, as the particular operative system that it is, shapes in its special fashion what he is aware of and knows and hence is capable of transmitting to others. or arrangement of parts into a whole which in turn is more than

Language *is* a system. A system is an orderly combination a conjunction, aggregate, or chance assembly of parts. As a system the parts or elements of a language constitute a whole and produce an over-all unity of function. More specifically, each language is a complex unique system with its own distinctive phonological, morphological, syntactical, lexical, and semantic organization. The particular language system is a mechanism which includes within itself and integrates the basically essential parts for complete human expression and communication. The standard sounds and combinations of sounds, the word forms, vocabulary, phrase and sentence structures have approximately the same signification for all members of the language community as these perform their central function of couching and transmitting the standardized meanings of all the types of situations to which they relate.

It is of special point, as the metalinguists have indicated, that language is the major medium for registering, indexing, categorizing, and recording human experience and culture and hence has a determining influence on all human perception and conceptualization and all social action and interaction.

Also of prime pertinence in the present analysis, each society has a self-contained meaning system (as can be inferred from chap. v). This meaning system embodies and summarizes all of the meanings already arrived at. The language system as a whole is the conveyor and depository of all of the meanings already arrived at by the society under its own unique complex of historical conditions. It is thus the established going medium through which its users interpret life and the world. As such it is a partial determinant of how and what they experience and comprehend, of how they think and what they think about, and of what is important and valuable and real for them.

The ultimate point of the discussion thus far is that the language system is a major determinant of what is funny in the society. It is the basic instrument for identifying, reflecting, expressing, embodying, and transmitting what is perceived and conceived as humorous or witty by the people of the language community. It affects what is laughed about and laughed at.

Indeed, it may be said to contain as well as determine the humor. Furthermore, its mutual comprehensibility aids in universalizing within the language community the expression and transmission of the humorous and witty. Its own structural forms and components provide unique manipulative possibilities and limits for creating and depicting humorous situations and evoking laughter.

A partial demonstration and proof of the uniqueness of each language system is that its inherent structural, semantic and stylistic elements, just noted above, cannot be reproduced with complete exactitude of form, meaning, and intent in any other language. This aspect of language is brought out in the circumstance that efforts to translate the humor and wit of one language into another is fraught with certain difficulties. In general, much humor as expressed in and by one language system for a given culture or nation cannot be accurately and precisely translated into humor and laughter for another, or even readily interpreted. Even at best it is likely that at least part of the comic element expressed will be lost.

There are certain structural linguistic complications of special significance. Each language has its own morphological intricacies; for example, different languages sometimes lack parallel parts of speech, thus making impossible the translation of a play on words. Particular designative words may have a sharply divergent connotation in another language—variant in what they refer to and what they categorize. Sentence structure may be quite different. It is difficult to translate metaphors, images, idioms. There is the possibility of what Leacock (84, 226) referred to as "a great vista of errors, mistakes, false genders, wrong plurals, mixed metaphors." Thus the humorous effects sought by the verbal techniques often do not carry through in the process of translation. A scientific statement can be much more accurately translated than can a joke or a pun.

2. LINGUISTIC HUMOR AND LAUGHTER

We are now concerned, not with the deterministic influence of the language system upon the humor and laughter of its

speakers, but with its converse—the humorus situations that arise
out of the employment of that complicated mechanism, language,
as an expressive and communicative instrument.

A. A language presents both verbal effectors and verbal
effects of humor. Many linguistic forms are, or can be, humorous
in themselves; and there are various linguistic situations and
occurrences that produce a comic state. Human beings realize
fun from language, have fun with language, and create fun by
means of language.

Such employment of language is quite to be expected. Language is the key operational factor in the daily life of a people;
it is almost as ubiquitous and pervasive as the atmosphere. The
people of the society are more involved in and occupied with this
basic institution than any other set of operational sociocultural
factors in their total lives. There is thus a likelihood of what
amounts to its comic misuse through ignorance, error, or in-
capacity by certain categories of people, of the efforts to manipulate relevant forms of it for humor-inducing ends due to its ready
availability, wide currency, and great diversity and wealth of
combinable components, of its continuous and general utilization
as an outlet for the expression of the sense of humor, and of the
deliberate ingenious creation of humorous linguistic forms. Long
historical experience demonstrates the effectiveness of these various linguistic products, forms, devices and techniques as laughter-
evoking means.

Linguistic situations are humorous for essentially the same
reasons as other types of situations. The humor and laughter
arises largely out of verbal incongruities: the departures from,
or exaggerations or violations of what is "standard" language for
the speakers exposed to the humor-arousing form and the thwarting of expectancies of standard form and usage; the switch of
meanings; the intrusion of the playful impulse in the juggling of
the language forms; the impracticality or illogicality of the particular term in the linguistic or social context; the opening of
heretofore non-existent or non-conventional vistas of meaning of
particular words or phrases; the amusement or confusion produced by either clever and ingenious or ignorant and stupid

specially created non-standard words, word combinations, and phrases; or other ludicrous deviations of structure, function, or meaning.[1]

The more widely appearing humorous linguistic forms will be briefly presented from the point of view of the unintentionality or intentionality of their employment as humorous devices by the actors. Some of the humor-eliciting linguistic forms are unintentional, or incidental, or even accidental. Others are intended by the performers and are deliberately manipulated and created as laugh getters. Most of them are both; that is, in some cases particular forms appear spontaneously in the type of social situation, and in others the same forms are deliberately imitated, appropriated, or fomented as devices for inducing humor into the situation and evoking laughter.[2]

B. Various mishaps and misuses in speech, writing, and printing, certain exaggerations and flamboyancies on the one hand and decreases and under-emphases on the other, and certain special-group modifications of usage produce humorous situations, largely of a ludicrous nature, that set the stage for mirth. We are concerned at this point with linguistic forms that *originally* occur unintentionally on the part of the performers of them in a given type of sociocultural situation or context. These forms are thought humorous by some of the population.

Various factors are responsible for the different, mainly unintentional, humor-eliciting forms. They may be due to the stupidity or fumbling and bumbling of the speakers or writers

---

[1] Bergson (115) wrote that in the sentence conveying the humorous ploy the ludicrous is usually created either by inversion—that is, the complete reversal of the natural or regular order of words or concepts; or by reciprocal interference of ideas in the sentence; or by transposition—that is, the changing of the natural expression of the idea into another key, or another way or level of understanding.

[2] For some earlier examinations of the relationship of language with wit and humor see Bergson, 103-131; Eastman, 1936: 115-145; Leacock, 11, 16-41, 83-84, 201-202, 226; Rapp, 1951: 73-108. For a monthly offering of excellent examples of current humorous linguistic perpetrations, both unintentional and deliberately contrived, see the column "Toward More Picturesque Speech" in the *Reader's Digest.*

of the non-standard forms, to their illiteracy or otherwise un-tutored state, to their limited acculturation, to their incomplete socialization, to the ecological specializations of speech within the larger language community, to the peculiar linguistic fabrications of ethnic groups, to the more or less unconscious resort to special exaltations, complications, and exaggerations of the language by certain special groups, even for some, aberrations of speech due to physical or psychological impairment. The limitations on accurate translation from one language to another produce occasional howlers and bloopers.

The following is a partial inventory of originally unintentional language behaviors that have stimulated mirth. The categories are not mutually exclusive.

1) Errors or slips in the use of the standard or conventional language: in grammar, vocabulary, spelling, sentence structure, pronunciation, and intonation, as, for example, on the part of small children, the ignorant or untutored, unassimilated immigrants, the disturbed or confused. These errors take many forms. Among them are the deviant words: distorted words, misused or wrong words, naïvely used words. The malapropism, a ridiculously or grotesquely incorrect or inappropriate use of a word or a phrase often is humorous: for example, "an allegory on the banks of the Nile," or (woman calling doctor) "My husband has the romantics," or "Lead the way and we'll precede." Mispronunciations are commonplace. Misspellings can create bizarre effects in meaning. Bad grammar either amuses or distresses the more knowledgeable.

2) Idiomatic mistakes and abuses, and some idiomatic allusions; for example, the mistakes of travelers in foreign lands, or the over-resort to the peculiarities of the language, causing the usage to be so odd or irregular as to be laughable in itself.

3) The overuse of metaphor, until the listener or reader laughs distractedly as he wonders what it's all about.

4) The unintentional droll word-play—slip of the tongue—of the spoonerism, that is, an accidental inversion of the sounds or syllables in two or more words, which creates a different phrase from the originally intended. For instance: a "half-warmed-

fish" for a "half-formed wish." In many instances the laughter is evoked because of the improper implications of the inverted phrase. A classic example is from Max Eastman (1936: 78): "The little old lady who went to church on Sunday morning, stepping quietly and soberly down the aisle, leaned over an elderly gentleman in one of the front rows, and asked him in a loud whisper: Is this pie occupewed?" Another is the comment: "It never pains but it roars."

5) Vernacular and colloquial speech, as distinct from formal or literary language, is often funny, even to its own users. This is the everyday speech, the familiar or "old shoe" below-standard language spoken in the common, repeated relationship of people and in the conduct of the widely shared activities of life, such as the sort of language we use when we go shopping, talk to the furnace repair man, speak familiarly and unrestrainedly to fellow family members or friends. It often expresses the speaker's wit and whimsy. It can be quite racy.

6) Some localisms and provincialisms of language are humorous to others. The common characteristic language forms of one community relating to peculiar local conditions or situations may be quite amusing to the people of other communities; for example, terms, subject-matters, and prevailing usages by farmers may be mirthfully enjoyed by city folks, and vice versa.

7) Much humor has been aroused among outsiders by the slangs, cants, jargons, and dialects of special-interest groups. These are special variants—corruptions in some respects—of the standard language: special in characteristic structural forms and/or in meaning, pronunciation, spelling. However, these may also be inflation and overdoing as the language is used.

Slang in general originates by more or less spontaneous generation on the part of particular groups or categories of speakers. It is language below the level of formal correctness of standard speech. Functionally, however, it consists of modifications of the language which make more effective in one way or another the specialized or secret communication and activity of the collective users. Slang may arouse laughter because of its inelegance, its unconventionality and grotesqueness, its exaggerated

imagery, its raciness, its startling exuberance; above all, it brusque
imagery, its raciness, its startling exuberance; above all, its
brusque departure from the commonplace, the stiff or stuffy,
the drab or trite.

The following are the more common special language forms—
in some instances sub-languages—characteristic of certain interest
groups or segments of the population that in some respects are
funny to some outsiders: (*a*) the special cants of the half-world
(e.g., circus folks, hoboes, pugilists) and the underworld (e.g.,
gangsters, criminals, dope pushers); (*b*) the jargons of some of
the crafts (e.g., jazz musicians, stage folk) and some of the
professions (e.g., esoteric scholarly or scientific language gone
berserk with six-syllable words, complicated and extended
technical vocabulary, and inflated phraseology that creates a
dense fog of words that defies efforts to transmit ideas and
produces either despair or laughter); (*c*) the mystic terminology
and semantics of such exotic groups as the hippies and yippies,
and new and perhaps ephemeral social movements; (*d*) the
eccentric speech of teen-agers and college students; (*e*) the
language of the sports (e.g., baseball, golf, especially when
transposed into other areas of interest); (*f*) dialects (sub-languages with peculiarities of vocabulary and idiom, accent, intonation and pronunciation, and grammatical forms, whether of specific regions, or social classes, or of racial segments of the population, or of ethnic groups) due to their grotesque forms and
seeming incongruities of usage supply targets for laughter for
the members of the standard language community of which the
dialect is a special phase. Closely related to ethnic-group dialect
as a laughter evoker is the brogue or other special pronunciation
of the standard language by the foreign-born.

8) Some euphemisms, subterfuges, and substitutes for oaths
are quite funny. One does not have to have a very sharp sense
of humor to smile when confronted with *male cow* for "bull,"
sanitation engineer for "garbage collector," *canine administrator*
for "dog catcher," or *therapeutic interruption of pregnancy* for
"voluntary abortion." The substitutes used in toning down the
moral inacceptability of expletives may be especially ludicrous;

for example, the clergyman's "Christopher Columbus" on the golf links as his drive hooks off into the deep rough. The very aura created by some euphemisms and subterfuges is apt to evoke laughter in the more realistic.

9) The unseemly speech, or the linguistic lapses from conventional and proper language of incumbents of particular social statuses are a long-standing evoker of laughter among the observers of such behavior. There is, for example, the adult talking in a childish manner ("baby talk"), the educated person speaking like a boor or a simpleton, the illiterate trying to speak in a "cultured" manner. Especially funny for many is the utterance of the person of exalted moral position when he slips from decorum, such as an expletive by the clergyman in the pulpit, or a vulgarism from a reputedly correct or refined person. If the lapse is shocking instead of amusing, it can produce the laughter of embarrassment.

10) Grandiose and grandiloquent language: the copious outpouring of hifalutin language on the part of a person is laughable for many when it is used in all seriousness, not to be funny but to be impressive. It consists in some extravagance or exaggeration for the particular person of vocabulary or rhetoric or style or enunciation. This is the "big words" and other show-off language of children, the language affectations of the inadequately tutored but zealous social climber, the flamboyant verbiage of the young M.D. trying to be imposingly scientific with his *auricular appendage* for "ear."

11) Typographical errors, editorial oversights, and copyreaders' misses have a humorous appeal for many. A small-town weekly provides the following public announcement: "The ladies of the Plum Street Church have discarded clothing of all kinds. They ask that you come and inspect them." A current events item: "Mrs. Alice Sommes, the club president, then rapped her navel and the meeting came to order."

12) Some translations and mistranslations are funny. Not only are there the metalinguistic difficulties in translating the humor and wit of one language into another, mentioned in section 1 above, but the translations themselves sometimes provide unin-

tended misrepresentations of meaning. The English "The spirit is willing but the flesh is weak" came out in Russian as 'The liquor is good but the food is bad." Translations of slang and colloquialisms may be so without flavor as to provide a laughter-evoking letdown.

13) Grotesque language performance due to physical or psychic defects or pathological states of the speakers evokes the laughter of some people, at least under certain circumstances and in certain company, as for example, the speech of persons with cleft palates or harelips, or paralytics, or that of stammerers, or that of drunken people. But such laughter is generally frowned upon.

14) Some catchwords and catchphrases (used to beguile, spellbind, stampede people) as employed in advertising, or by religious or political persuaders, are so ridiculous that they in themselves or in the context in which they are used, evoke derisive laughter.

15) Some neologisms are ridiculous because they are fancy names for quite commonplace and familiar objects and processes.

16) Verbosity itself—a muchness of language, a blitz of words—may be funny to many: A man who lisped was telling an acquaintance about a third man who "talked and talked and talked!" The acquaintance asked: "What did he talk about?" The lisped reply: "He didn't thay!"

C. Linguistic forms and meanings deliberately created for humorous ends. We are now concerned with the fact—the reverse of the immediately preceding discussion—that the institutionalized language of the society is subjected to conscious and deliberate verbal and semantic manipulation and formulation to achieve comic, or humorously quaint, striking, or startling linguistic situations that evoke laughter. Such behavior stems from the desire of many people to be amusing, or especially expressive, or to have the delight of exploration and invention, or to show off a bit. Professional humorists engage in such activity to entertain people at a profit. It involves some intelligence, imagination, knowledge, ingenuity and finesse in the verbal and semantic manipulation of the language, and in occasional instances the creation of new types of linguistic situations that produce structural and semantic laughter-evoking incongruities. To put it simply, it consists in having fun with language.

The major forms of deliberate production of humorous linguistic forms involve verbal trickery and stunting, especially a play on words, a creation of bizarre new words, a distortion of words, or a combination of words that gives a humorous contradiction or juxtaposition of meanings. The following are well-known forms.

1) Puns, which exist in every language, are probably also the most frequently and widely used technique for the purposeful perpetration of humorous linguistic situations among us. They originate in the fact that in every language words are created which have the same sound but differ in sense. The pun consists of the witty use of two words having the same or similar sounds (e.g., "scent" and "cent") but different meanings or applications, or of two different more or less incongruous meanings of the same word (e.g., to "pin" something on somebody). It is a playing on, or a manipulation of, the sounds and the nuances of meaning of words (Davis, 2-3, 102, 200; Eastman, 1936: 115-131; Girdansky, 113-116; Rapp, 1951: 87-100).

Punning requires considerable natural ability, vivacity, special facility in the use of the lexicon and semantics of the language, and a substantial sense of humor. While what amounts to an occasional instance among children, only rarely is a pun likely to appear as a mistake or an accident among adults.

Examples: (*a*) "One swallow does not make a summer, nor quench the thirst." (*b*) A joke quoted by Freud: "Have you taken a bath?" "No. Why? Is there one missing?" (*c*) A man about an acquaintance with very different life interests: "All we have in common is some common stock in XYZ Company." (*d*) The old saw: "The effect of the moon on the tide and the untied." (*e*) An Oliver Wendell Holmes' Yankee witticism: "Put not your trust in money, but put your money in trust." (*f*) Chief Justice Marshall coined this doublebarreled one: "The corn was full of kernels and colonels full of corn." (*g*) "You can't teach an old gnu new tricks." (*h*) "A lot of credit cards are being sent where no credit is due."

Puns have had considerable use in history. Some of our greatest humorists (e.g., Mark Twain, Ring Lardner, Ogden Nash) have been master punsters.

2) Condensed words—the fusion of two words into a witty condensation—are occasionally resorted to.

Freud (15) gives us the example from Heine's *Reisebilder* in which the precious character, Hirsch-Hyacinth, sat next to Solomon Rothschild: "who treated me (i.e., Hirsch-Hyacinth) just as if I were his equal, quite *famillionaire.*"

Recent examples: *alcoholidays*—holidays conducive to alcoholic indulgence; *anecdotage*—an affliction of old age; *protestrian* —a demonstrator marching; *Castrophobia*—a maldisposition of air travelers to the southeast of the United States.

3) Bon mots, those pat and clever words or expressions for given situations, often intentionally witty, pop up in almost every group of bright people, such as Elbert Hubbard's "The path of civilization is paved with tin cans," or the more recent "Eat, drink, and be merry, for tomorrow ye diet." Closely related are the wisecracks: "People who live in glass houses shouldn't!" or "A tax cut is the kindest cut of all."

4) The humorous term or phrase used (or created) as a form of critical characterization: "He's not a singer, he's a voca-lamity."

5) Clever metaphorical terms for well-known things are concocted for humorous ends. Thus we have waffles presented as "non-skid pancakes"; Artemus Ward called the American eagle "patriotic poultry."

D. The intentional use of many originally unintentionally humorous linguistic forms. Experience with a considerable number of humorous forms of speech appearing quite spontaneously or "naturally" in different types of sociocultural situations has shown them to be so effective as laugh-getters that they have been and are now deliberately appropriated by amateur humorists and employed by many of us in our daily interaction. The professional humorists, comedians, and showmen have also made wide use of them.

1) Typical mishaps or misuses are imitated. Bad grammar is used to make fun. Artemus Ward (Charles Farrar Brown) coined the word "ingrammaticisms" to describe such ways of making language funny. Almost every form of ingrammaticism condemned as bad by those of serious taste has been used by our comic writers as a source of witty expresion. Petroleum V. Nasby (David Ross Locke) and Jack Billings (H. W. Shaw) used the phonetic spelling of language as pronounced by the common man with telling effect.

2) Racy vernacular is deliberately concocted by both the amateur and the professional (e.g., Artemus Ward and Ring Lardner).

3) Slang in itself is engaged in just for the fun of it—as an exercise in wit or humor; for example, as it provides humorous (*old soak*) or facetious (*gink* or *bird* for "man") connotations, or other droll or spicy ways of saying things or portraying situations. Some slang starts as the linguistic ingenuity and whimsicality of one individual: G. B. Shaw, Ring Lardner, Walter Winchell. Some of it, for example the slang of teen-agers and college students, of some of the half-world and underworld, is developed as a protest against the restraints imposed by formality and convention. It shows new possibilities in words as it produces terms and meanings for which the standard tongue has no expression.

4) Dialects and brogues have also been widely appropriated by American humorists in the past (e.g., by Artemus Ward's "Mr. Dooley" and "Mr. Hennessey," Ring Lardner). However, those of the immigrant ethnic stocks (Italian, Scottish, Irish, Jewish, German, Swedish) have been rapidly diminishing since the nineteen twenties due to the complete assimilation of the collectivities speaking them.[3] The internal localisms, provincialisms, and sectional dialects are also in process of disappearance,

---

[3] That hardy perennial, "The Katzenjammer Kids" comic strip, is a conspicuous exception.

except among some voluntarily socially isolated groups, as the result of the linguistic uniformation of the different localities and regions brought about by mass communication and inter-areal mobility of the people.

5) Euphemisms and other substitutes for more offensive forms are often intentionally given a humorous turn. Hell is spoken of as a "warm climate," death as "pushing up the daisies" or "kicking the bucket." The names of places where the excretory functions are exercised are especially prone to such tinkering. The ladies' rest room—itself a euphemism—may be designated as the powder room, or more racily as the Heifers' Corral. The men's rest room may be archly referred to as the Little Boys' Room.

6) Hifalutin language usually brings a laugh if the audience knows it is simulated. The professional comedian finds it sure-fire entertainment. Everyday practitioners often use it to show up a show-off.

XVII. Humor and Laughter and the Mass Media

The mass aspects of modern society are among its most conspicuous features. We are confronted with a mass society, with its mass communication directed to mass audiences by means of the mass media and presumably producing social psychological, sociocultural, and societal massing. The massing agents, with their massing effects, have profoundly affected laughter both as a form of communication and as a social product. In this chapter we are especially concerned with the part the mass media play in evoking laughter in the modern world, the nature of the mass audience to which the humorous efforts of the media are directed, the effects on the forms of laughter of this mass communication, the variant reception by the different segments of the public, and the effects on the standards and patterns of behavior of the population.

1. PRESENT-DAY MASS HUMOR

The new mass media of communication have a tremendous effect on the members of modern communities as they add new dimensions and increased scope and volume to communication. They include a variety of technologically developed impersonal media such as printed matter, especially in the form of newspapers, mass magazines, best-seller fiction, and comic strips and comic books, popular music records, motion pictures, radio, television, billboards, placards, much advertising, even skywriting. Almost all of us are subjected to the influence of these visual, literary, graphic, or auditory media during much of our daily waking hours; indeed, there is almost no escaping them. They provide most of our information, regulation and propaganda.

Of special moment, they also provide the people with much of their diversion, entertainment, and recreation. This function is to create relaxation, respite from duties, to provide enjoyment and enable people to forget their worries, to fill leisure or idle time, and to offer an escape from boredom. The presentation of comic and humorous situations and the stimulation of laughter is probably the most important and widespread type of procedure in this entertainment and amusement. The mass media are thus the source of much of the humor to which moderns have access or to which they are exposed.

That audio-visual medium, television, as an influence on the American people, including its use in evoking laughter, is especially significant. It is said that the average American spends about one-third of his waking time in watching TV. Some of the name programs are viewed by millions upon millions. Says Surgeon General William Stewart of the United States Public Health Service, "By age 16 the average American child has spent more hours in front of a TV set than in the classroom." The American people are getting more and more of their entertainment from TV, and less and less from the stage and movie theaters. It is estimated (Schulman, 124) that two-thirds of TV shows are devoted to Westerns and action-adventure and one-third to comedy. Television has come to be the most nearly omnipresent medium for the spread of humor. Writers of humor and professional comics must turn to it in greater and greater numbers for a hearing (Schulman, 122).

2. THE NATURE OF THE MASS AUDIENCE

The mass media operate in a mass society with its huge, widespread, and heterogeneous population, and direct their humorous and laugh-provoking efforts to a phase of mass society of special significance from the point of view of communication, namely, the mass audience. The mass audience, that is, the entire body of potential recipients of the communicative thrust within the transmitive range of the media, is thus the demographic, social psychological and societal body within which the laughter occurs. This vast collectivity has important effects on the individual and social functions performed by the laughter occurring in it.

What are its pertinent features? A mass audience may number in the millions, usually widely scattered geographically, socially and psychically separated and isolated, impersonally related, and usually unorganized, or very loosely organized. When the members are exposed to or receive any given message, whether by literary or graphic device, by radio or TV, they are alone or part of a very small informal, even happenstantial group, or they are discrete and anonymous atoms in a secondary-group mass relationship.

Furthermore the audience is not necessarily an amorphous mass of more or less identical individuals. Usually it is heterogeneous and diversified, consiting of many population elements dissimilar in interests, convictions, sensitivities, tastes, knowledge, capacity for reception, and behavioral response. The mass audience may be said to consist of numerous and diverse subaudiences.

These sub-audiences read or view or listen to what they are interested in and what they agree with; they ignore or avoid what they are not interested in or not capable of being interested in, or what is not congenial with their prior attitudes, habits, beliefs, and ideas. This means selectivity.

3. THE RELEVANT FEATURES OF THE MASS MEDIA AFFECTING LAUGH-PROVOKING TECHNIQUES AND ATTITUDES

Mass communication, regardless of the content, form, or purpose of the message presented, is conducted, in the main, by vast profit-making corporate organizations to influence unorganized audiences. As transmitting agents these have a single, centralized, or monopolized control over the selection and production of the laugh (and other) materials and their transmission. Much of what the media utilize and distribute is the output of the fun-making industry referred to in Chapter VII, section 4.

The media also, quite understandably, seek a huge volume of output and a massive impact. Consequently, they try to catch as many purchasers, subscribers, attenders, listeners, viewers as possible.

They are confronted, however, with individual differentials in laughter capabilities, interest, and appeal discussed in Chapter VI, section 3, and the heterogeneous and diversified nature of the mass audience just noted. This imposes a special task upon the mass media. In order to bring about maximum exposure and widest response to the "fun exhibitions" they try to make all sorts of appeals, for all sorts of people, under all sorts of circumstances and at different times and occasions. One well-known tactic is to appeal to very broad interest sectors of the population; for example, the pointing of some of the Sunday supplement comic strips especially to children. Another is to devote themselves to laughter universals (chap. v), in which case the producers have to meet the specifications of the principle of the greatest common denominator.

4. THE STRATEGIC IMPACT OF THE LAUGH-PROVOKING MESSAGES ON THE MASS AUDIENCE

Now that we have a proper background, let us focus attention on certain social psychological and sociological factors affecting the mass audience recipients of the transmitted message and the effects of these factors on them.

A. In the first place, the recipients are trapped targets. The message is consciously designed and produced for the purposes of the senders and is transmitted to the intended potential consumers through the established organizationally controlled channels. The members of the audience have not arranged for or chosen the form or content of the communication that they get from the corporate creators and distributors. What they have thrust at them is both a sort of handout and a channeled product.

The targets have been described as sitting ducks or captives. They must take the message as it is, or else turn it off.

B. A second aspect, closely related to the first, is that the communication of the message, in mass communication, regardless of its content or purpose, is almost exclusively one-way. There is very little reciprocal communication or exchange of experience. Communication by means of the mass media is not the two-way, three-way, or many-way interaction of the dyad, triad, or larger groups of face-to-face associates. Of course, the reciprocity of communication as between performer and audience even in the direct contact, face-to-face audience is seldom entirely free and equal. Many members of such audiences do not directly exchange reaction with the performance, and some types of such audiences do not permit such exchange. But the communication between agent and audience in the case of mass communication, in its very nature, is only, and can be only, from the sending organization to the separate atoms of the mass.

This produces a special situation. Face-to-face communication is directly and immediately reciprocal between receiver and sender; it permits completely symmetrical feedback—a free-flow reaction or response or "comeback" from the receiver back to the sender. But in mass communication there can be no instantaneous dialogue. The recipient cannot react back directly and immediately, and the sender cannot assess the reaction to his message or performance.

There is no direct effect upon and no immediate feedback to the creator or performer of the humorous incident of the reactions of the audience. It cannot talk back or laugh back to affect the flow of the laugh-production, or to enable the sensing of the present approval or disapproval of the members. The determining of the response of the audience comes later, by means of such checking devices as the Nielsen ratings of TV programs, and the evidence of increase, steady maintenance, or perceptible decline or withdrawal of patronage or purchase or attendance of the audience. And such tests affect only possible future performances.

The actual view of the comedian on the TV screen as he

performs may diminish the non-reciprocal element somewhat, but the communication is still one-way. Jackie Gleason or an Ed Sullivan performer cannot tell how *I* react to his antics.

Because mass communication is largely one-way, it may actually discourage response, especially the desire to react back or to join in or follow suit. It is also possible that the one-way aspect has been a factor in the occasionally mentioned increased passivity, apathy, and inarticulateness of the people, to be discussed in the concluding chapter.

C.   The humorous or other message is from a single source and addressed to the "public". The single speaker or writer or cartoonist or the personnel producing the particular program submit a message *to* very many people. The humorous situation presented is not a spontaneous cooperative expression of interest or creativeness, on the part of the people whose laughter response is sought and possibly aroused. Thus we have the likely tremendous influence of a single source transmitting a single message simultaneously to millions upon millions of people who are largely faceless and nameless spectators. Indeed, much of the mass-media laughter could appropriately be called spectator laughter, in contrast to participant laughter. The laughers are functionally separated from the humorous or comic event they are laughing at; they have no part in its inception or precipitation, its procedure, or its outcome; they only receive.

D.   Due to the mechanized nature of very much of it, it lacks much social and socializing effect. Mass communicated laughter is mechanically spread among people in indirect and media-provided contact. The mass audience itself as we have noted, is composed of people without direct contact and exchange with each other. The members are spatially, psychically, and socially separated. Millions may be laughing simultaneously at the same induced humorous situation, but it is a mechanically induced rather than a socially induced sociopsychological phenomenon. It may in fact be in part a response to the mechanically created suggestiveness of the dubbed-in laughter of the sound track of the movie, or the radio or TV broadcast.

The upshot is that this laughter induced in physical and

social isolates loses much of its shared and reverberating effect. Without direct personal contact there is little of the infectiousness or imitativeness of laughter that one finds in a face-to-face group.

Even the movie audience, though its members are physically together, is mainly impersonal. There may be frequent common laughter induced by some comic act on the screen, or humorous sally on the sound track, but it is a mechanically produced, not sociopsychically joined, laughter.

E.   In spite of the diversities in the subaudiences and in the receptiveness of their members the recipients nevertheless are mightily conditioned and shaped by what they are exposed to and submit to. Because the media are monopolistic, the audience have no choice but to take what they get from the great corporate creators and mass distributors of much of our humor. The mass media can thus mold the humor awarenesses and interests of millions of consumers. While they supposedly provide what the public is interested in or wants, at any given time they set the laughter themes and spirit and the moral standards of the programs, and in some measure determine the tastes and sensitivities regarding what is funny and laughable. This, of course, directly affects the standards and patterns of behavior of the population.

XVIII. Laughter in the Modern World

A final analysis of the social scientific aspects of laughter is concerned with laughter as it operates in the modern world. Any such examination, however cursory, raises a host of questions. A major one is: What is happening to laughter today? or more specifically, how is laughter being affected by recent sociopsychological and sociocultural changes? These questions immediately suggest a number of correlate, subsidiary, and tangential questions that will be dealt with in the ensuing discussion. This review will also have another, though largely incidental, effect, namely, to exemplify some of the factors affecting the social climate of laughter, particularly the conditions favorable and unfavorable to it.

Compatibly with the principles set forth in Chapter V, there have been marked changes in laughter themes; some have disappeared and some are new—characteristic of the present moment. There seem to have been considerable changes in the social awareness of and social concern about situations that might be deemed to be humorous. There have thus also been marked changes in many of the things which are strictly of the present, as compared with the past, which professional humorists are making fun of. There seemingly have been changes in choral, public, and mass laughter, in the contagiousness of laughter, and in the social display of humor. Marked changes in the public media for inducing laughter, especially in the way of the popularity and the circulation-exposure influence of the different kinds of mass media have occurred.

The changes involved in these surmises are intricately and

reciprocally interrelated. Information about them is limited; the student of laughter thus cannot yet support most of them positively with scientifically established facts and conclusions. Nonetheless, several areas of tentative generalization with a great likelihood of substantive validity loom up. Each set of generalizations, however, applies only within specific limits and in particular types or situations, or in particular and specifically qualified frames of reference. Therefore, some of the generalizations may seem at first glance to be contradictory or inconsistent with each other.

1.   THE CASE FOR MORE UNIVERSAL LAUGHTER

As far back as 1935, Leacock (202) pointed to the possibility of an increase in laughter universals in our present kind of world. There is every likelihood that many long-standing common-human and common-cultural laughter themes that cut across sociological context lines will continue to prevail. These relate to universal and continuous human interests and concerns and provide situations which strike most people as humorous.

The spread of modern technologies and particularly the vastly extended areal range of the modern means of communication, and the vastly increased inter-people mobility and contact are making for a considerable degree of cultural uniformation, and the development of an increasing number of common, universal cultural elements. The situation is reflected to some extent in the universalization of some interests and the related laughter themes, and of the nation-wide and even world-wide extension of certain laughters.

Within a nation or society, as noted in Chapter V, there are many common themes. Each society has its own distinctive character. This accounts for the great similarity of action and reaction of the individuals and subcultures in the most typical and recurrent social situations. But these distinctive features and conditions also create the setting and context for the common humorous situations within the society.

I have examined two widely circulated types of American

laughter-inducing materials for the recurring laughter themes. First are some thirty issues of the syndicated comic strips appearing with the *Lincoln Sunday Journal and Star* scattered through the period August, 1967, to June, 1969. The weekly collection is offered as "The World's Greatest Comics." The strips, of course, are not now entirely devoted to the comic or the funny. Second is a rather extensive sampling of jokes from the syndicated columns of jokes by American professional jokesters appearing regularly in the Sunday supplement *Parade* extending over about the same period as the strips. Both the strips and the columns appear in many American newspapers and are representative of their kind the country over. The readership of the strips and jokes is as diversified as that of the general public reading the newspapers in which they appear. The people come from all types of homes and cultural backgrounds and vary in intelligence and educational attainment. It can be surmised that since the media are obviously devised to be comical or funny, they reflect phases of contemporary life which are of humorous interest to large segments of the population—phases that produce mirth across regional, social class, even ethnic group lines.

There are such recurent themes as the following: (1) status differentials: tactics of social climbers, foibles of the *nouveaux riches;* (2) television: jocularity about programs, commercials, ways of life in connection with TV; (3) auto driving: traffic problems and experiences, parking problems, arguments with cops and other drivers, backing and parking antics of women; (4) family and marital situations: husband and wife episodes, family deception tactics, fussy housekeeping, funny acts of children, teen-agers' and women's addictions such as telephone talkathons, kids leaving toys on the floor and bikes in the driveway, outdoor cooking by dad, parents advising children, mother-in-law problems, henpecked husbands, bad habits of either spouse, kids "borrowing" or overusing the family car, hippie antics of teen-age offspring; (5) poking fun at American things and ways: breakfast foods, food fads, vitamins, gadgetry (electric toothbrushes, dishwashers, etc.); (6) mental health, psychiatry, psychiatrists; (7) the space, atom, and fission age: outer space, living on the moon, "fishing by satellite"; (8) in the mail: bills, requests for contributions, junk; (9) political quips and parodies: about politics, politicians, public officials, government employments, taxes; (10) financial inflation: effects on family purchasing and consumption;[1] (11) weather bureau failures in prediction;[2] (12) overactivity of old (retired) people; (13) women in search of beauty: beauty-shop episodes, weight watching; (14) smart-alecks; (15) hippies, yippies, and beatniks: acts, attire, ways;[3] (16) seasonal activities: snow shoveling, gardening, vacation exploits; (17) economic concerns: inflation, credit cards.[4]

Another aspect involves the exposure to the nation-wide, even international, mass media transmitting humor and provoking laughter discussed in the preceding chapter. While some of their messages appeal to special sectors of the population, in their rather distinctive and well-known forms, they have unmistakable universalizing effects. In the United States we have the widespread mass laughter of far-flung audiences such as (1) the millions ranging from dropouts to Ph.D.'s that watch and/or listen to the antics and patter of nation-wide, even internationally, favorite entertainers and comedians; (2) the millions upon millions of people who consume the millions upon millions of comic books published each year, and those who daily, and with a multi-barreled treat on Sunday, devour the just-mentioned comic strips; (3) the more select but still numerous readers of the daily and weekly press who laugh at the widely circulated accounts of the political blunders, or clever, or laughable acts of statesmen

---

[1] Outer space and inflation were combined in both a comic strip and a prize joke: a refutation of the general argument that the dollar doesn't go as far as formerly, namely, "It goes to India, and Formosa, and Egypt, and Pakistan, and South America, and even outer space."

[2] As one joke would have it, the weather bureau should call itself a "non-prophet organization."

[3] Examples: "In the old days a boy would give his girl his class ring when they were going steady. Nowadays, he lets her use his hair curlers." (By Totie Fields.) About the beatnik wedding: "They gave the bride a shower before the wedding."

[4] For a study of dominant themes and major goals of Sunday comic strips between 1943 and 1958 see Francis E. Barcus, *The World of Sunday Comics*, in White & Wells, 190-218.

or other conspicuous persons; (4) the wider audiences that enjoy the highly popular and widely syndicated cartoons, satirical columns, and collections of jokes.

Conditions exist today which are conducive to the development of world-wide uniformities in what is judged comic or otherwise laughable. There is a seemingly increasing world-wide standardization of some tastes and interests and situations due to the modern technologies of mass communication, mass production, distribution, advertising, and consumption, and to the increasing and areally extending mobility of people and things, increasing urbanization, mass leisure, mass entertainment and amusement, mass art, and even mass government. Theoretically these can, and actually to some extent they do, create common situations prevailing over great areas that inevitably produce common types of humorous reactions.

As a result of such uniformation there are appearing in many parts of the world jokes and other expressions about humorous aspects of urban life (crowding, traffic snarls, etc.); about gadgetry and new technicways; about attire (with the universalizing of wearing apparel, e.g., miniskirts); about universal societal structural relations (e.g., class stratification, always a rich area for satirical humor); jokes relating to world-wide games and sports. There is the distinct possibility that a global mass humor is appearing in such departments of modern life.

The messages of some of the media, for example, radio and TV, can instantly transcend political barriers and physical space and thus affect millions upon millions of people. They can be said to provoke universal instant laughter.

2. THE CASE FOR LESS UNIVERSAL LAUGHTER

There is the other side of the coin. Internationally the world-wide uniformizing forces and structures are producing common laughter themes as just noted. But each nation and society also has its own numerous cultural differences in contrast to the other nations and societies; and this results in a large body of indigenous laughter themes. The proliferation of new nations, each seeking distinctive identity and "presence" in the world, could well lead to deliberate fostering of "national" *cultural* themes on their part, and thus, in turn, to the creation of new and diverse *laughter* themes.

In the first place, many of the uniformities and uniformations of taste, interest, and behavior produced by the mass-effect technologies are merely *surface* similarities and conformities. With just a little penetration below the surface one finds an almost unbelievable sociocultural diversity among the different segments of the population. We Americans, for example, are a pluralistic society, which means that we consist of a multiplicity of diverse collectivities with a variety of values, interests, prejudices, and objectives. Also, in the same connection, much of the more meaningful, satisfying, and determinative association of people *is* as members of ever-more inclusive and restricted collectivities. These conditions affect laughter.

Within the United States, though much of this applies to most of the "advanced" nations or societies, there seems to be some evidence of less universal and less widely joined laughter. So much of the joined laughter that we do have seems to be more and more segmental, diversified, and particularistic; it is laughter confined to specific population segments or subcultures and relates to their peculiar life-situations. We may be trending toward more laughter sects.

This differentiation of laughter seems to stem from several related conditions: diversities of interests between collectivities, audiences, and publics, due in part at least to differences in educational level, in type and degree of cultural sophistication, in social class, in occupation, and in age group; limited social psychic contact and some degree of sociocultural isolation of these segments from each other; the impersonalness of much of the contact between the segments, which is not conducive to reciprocal stimulation of laughter or of joined or choral laughter.

Much of such widespread choral or mass laughter as we do have is not that of members of a face-to-face pack or herd with its directly perceptible presure and exchange; but that of impersonally related and scattered millions exercising the take-it-

or-leave-it option regarding the messages of the mass media of communication. This may be thought of as social laughter, but it is largely one-way and not reciprocal. It is, on the one hand, the private laughter of people responding as discrete members of vast audiences; on the other, the choral laughter of different diffused masses.

This impersonal nature of the association and communication among the potential joined laughers also greatly limits the contagiousness of the laughter, even among those with common social and cultural interests.

With the vast amount of hostility and belligerency in the modern world, there also seems to be less joined laughter as an expression of group triumph or of contempt. It might be surmised, incidentally, that the present offers fewer widely and consciously felt great national accomplishments to unite all population elements in joyous or triumphant laughter.

Due to various differentials in the laughable, especially between cultures, subcultures and localities, there probably has been and today is more laughing together at other cultures, subcultures, and localities than laughing with them; for example, the communist world laughing at the non-communist world, and vice versa; Asiatics laughing at Europeans and Americans, the squares of the bourgeois world laughing with each other at the beats and hips of the bohemian world and vice versa; the younger generation laughing at the older and vice versa.

3. THE CASE FOR LESS LAUGHTER

We have no records of the amount of laughter in given types of social situations in the past. Nor do we have established criteria or techniques for testing the amount of laughter engaged in by the members of a society, either past or present.[5] The impression of studious observers is that laughter, like out-

---

[5] There are, of course, the laugh meters used by the motion-picture, radio, and TV industries to register the volume of audience response to particular humorous productions. We are here concerned with a comparison of the laughter prevailing in a given community or society at different historical periods.

door whistling, has been diminishing in recent and present society. As early as 1902, Sully (2) stated that ". . . in these latter days the band of laughers has dwindled."[6] Gregory (96) reports that it has been contended that "in the early ages of this world there was far more laughter than is to be heard now."

On the basis of some knowledge of historical American social life, and direct observations as a professional social scientist extending over more than a half century, I have the definite impression that contemporary people, both as individuals and as collectivities, do less laughing in most social situations than was done in earlier periods of our history. I do not mean that people are losing their sense of humor or that the humorous spirit and laughter are dying out in the United States. There are still plenty of common-interest and face-to face situations, especially in the family and between friends or other close acquaintances, in which laughter is free and abundant (though there is a possibility of shrinkage of even such laughter). Many impersonal interactional occasions involving common interest and experience, quite a few of them of a "public" nature, do now and will continue to provoke it. People, individually and collectively, still enjoy a burst of rollicking mirth. The humorous spirit is still awake and productive. Laughter will not disappear as long as human beings communicate. But sociocultural and sociopsychological changes have altered—even eliminated—certain types of situations, and which have modified awareness of, interest in, and attitudes toward what have been deemed to be more or less standard humorous situations. These have diminished general mirthfulness.

Below are briefly indicated forms of laughter that are declining and what seem to be valid factors in their decline.

A. There are many more people and more contacts, but more impersonal interaction, more sociopsychological isolation (aloneness), and less interpersonal meaning conveyance. A

---

[6] In the concluding pages of his study (427-432) Sully, from the perspective of 1902, discusses the decline of different forms of laughter, including the social and sociopsychological factors responsible for the changes.

greater number of people are ever more crowded; and contacts with others have increased since a century ago. A modern urbanite, for example, has some sort of contact or joint presence with thousands in a day. But these thousands are more and more anonymous, and the contacts more and more impersonal and mechanical; there is less person-to-person communication; often there is an avoidance of communication between casually associating persons. The contacts are such as merely passing on the street, or jointly occupying an elevator, or occupying space together in a store or theater; or they are the highly formalized contacts of customer and saleslady, customer and bank clerk—the impersonal and personally inconsequential contacts of the modern megalopolis. Other contacts are those provided by the mass media of communication and entertainment, but among people physically and psychically isolated from each other.

The contacts are not the kind that foster interpersonal understandings; they provide less and less feelingful interaction with associates. In fact, the social warmth of contact has diminished with the increasing impersonality of that contact. Many people are sociopsychologically more alone than were their ancestors; they are increasingly strangers to one another. People have fewer close acquaintances with whom to share the euphoria of laughter.

It is of key importance that laughter emerges from meaningful contact with others. The person who is physically or sociopsychologically alone is less likely to laugh as a means of individual release or expression. Even more pertinent, a large number of modern individuals have meaning-conveying communication with only a few of the many people with whom they are in contact, or only the most fleeting and superficial meaning conveyance. Indeed, they have very limited meanings to convey by laughter.

Note that with the impersonal nature of the contacts, the reverberating and infectious nature of laughter may be lost; in fact, some people seem deliberately to repress any show of concern, resentment, or amusement. Finally, with so much alienation of people from each other, many are likely not to share conceptions of the humorous with each other.

We moderns are less and less concerned with the affairs and actions or even the presence of those other persons whom we pass on the street or jostle in the elevator. There is a feeling of distance from them, an increasing obtuseness regarding them, and an ever-more callous disregard of them. What they do is "their own business," "none of my business"; "I couldn't care less!" As a result it seems that there is less interpersonal laughter, either friendly or hostile. As individuals we laugh less *with* others; we do not even bother to laugh *at* them.[7]

B. Change is blunting the sense of incongruity. Today with so much change, so many varieties of change, and such rapid change, people are becoming inured to change. Many occurrences coming with technological, ideological, and behavioral change, however bizarre, exceptional, incomprehensible, illogical, improbable, or presumably impossible—and theoretically creating the basic laughter situation of incongruity when they do occur —do not arouse laughter any more. What once might have been experienced as a ludicrous juxtaposition of elements no longer seems to be.

The "unexpected" has lost much of its effect: almost anything can now be expected. Situations formerly presenting seeming incongruities have now come to be viewed as commonplace realities and standard expectancies. Even if a bit of incongruity still lingers regarding some situation for some person, it at best produces only a smile or a smirk.

It is also possible that the diversification of sociocultural interests as well as the superficial nature of much of the effect of the massing agents is not conducive to the maintenance of those uniform and shared fundamental understandings that enable people to detect incongruities, contradictions, and illogicalities.

---

[7] This increasing impersonality of relations can have an important social control effect. It may weaken or neutralize the critical weight or corrective effect of the accusatory laughter of other individuals or groups. The potential accusers do not know the possible culprit; they do not care about him unless they are immediate and obvious suffering victims of him. They do not laugh at or against him. He himself is lost in the mass unless he is a spotlight person at the particular moment, and can escape detection, accusation, and punishment.

Our very cosmopolitanism and pluralism may be bringing about a diminishing awareness of and attention to differences, even an insensibility to them.

C. People are so lacking in knowledge regarding many situations that they cannot or do not assay them as humorous. Many contemporary human affairs are too complicated and turbulent to be readily comprehended or understood. Many people are puzzled and baffled by them. They have so little knowledge about many of these ever-different and new conditions that they do not recognize them as possibly having contradictory, or disorderly, or unusual, or eccentric, or deviant aspects. Some people have come to believe almost anything—or nothing.

Some ignore the baffling occurrences ("I don't give a damn!" or "What the hell!"); in others it produces a state of apathy or indifference ("So what?"); still others accept whatever occurs as part of the new overwhelming, unfathomable, inevitable "state of things" ("We gotta take it!")[8]

Both the inurement to change and the increasing lack of interpretative knowledge regarding events reduce the likelihood of laughter. People are not startled any more by much that is new and strange and incomprehensible. There is no surprise, hence no occasion for surprise release, no reduction or easing of nervous, mental, or emotional tension.

D. The standardizing effect on behavior of the mass media has caused some laughters to diminish. The mass media of communication, especially TV, tend to standardize the emotions, interests, tastes, attitudes, feelings, and thoughts of millions upon millions in many situations. Indeed, many of these millions ob-

---

[8] Winick (1964) has noted that there seems to have been a decline of satire in writers and artists of the present century. They do not seem to have responded to its use as did, for example, Mark Twain, Thorstein Veblen, Kin Hubbard, E. W. Howe, and Sinclair Lewis. He notes also the passing of an imposing number of satirical magazines—Puck, the old *Life*, *Judge*, *Vanity Fair*, *American Mercury*, and *Ballyhoo*. The *New Yorker*, originally a satirical magazine, now has only a diminishing portion of satirical or even humorous content. He implies that a main reason may be that today's adult world is so normless or so confused about norms that it "cannot respond to an art form that implicitly is based on departures from the norm."

tain the greater proportion of the content of their emotions, ideas, and overt actions from the mass media. The effect is to induce mental and social behavior among much of the population that is collectivized, stereotyped, canalized, even automatized, and which is, in turn, more and more universalized. But as in inurement to change and the increasing lack of interpretative knowledge, this very universalization of behavior can lead not only to less universal laughter but to less laughter in general. This is because more and more people are engaged in standard and similar behavior which, because it is so widespread and common, is not funny or otherwise laughter-evoking save to the greatly eccentric or the keenly critical and objective.

E. Paradoxical though it may seem in the light of the possible circumstance just discussed, the very increase of formal education for considerable portions of the population may be conducive to some restriction of general laughter by diminishing the laughter situations for some of the educated. First, it is possible that while the type of higher education pursued by some may diversify and extend their interests, the type pursued by others—probably a majority—may specialize them. It might then have the effect of making many of the more educated more selective, particularized, and exclusive in what they conceive and react to as humorous, and narrow their range of laughables. Second, it is possible that many of the more highly educated people take a more realistic and discerning attitude toward much of life, see fewer aspects of it as peculiar, or ludicrous, or incongruous as compared with the lesser educated, and therefore do not laugh so much or so unrestrainedly.

F. Some social situations, until recently generating much humor, no longer arouse or permit laughter. Social changes of a structural-functional nature and changes in social values and attitudes (cf. chap. v, secs. 3, 5) seem to be diminishing certain social situations or relations as laughter themes. In the United States the laughter evoked by most of our ethnic groups—Irish, Scottish, Swedish, German, Jewish, etcetera—has markedly declined. We see few jokes now about their typical funny ways of action and thought as compared with the huge volume of these a half century ago; their dialects and brogues are no longer used for humorous purposes (Dudden, 35). The prime reason, of course, as previously noted, is that the assimilation of the nineteenth-century immigrant stocks is virtually complete. Their descendants are an indistinguishable part of the general homogenized citizenry.

Since World War II, but especially during the past decade, racial humor, especially making fun of or about Negroes, has practically disappeared after being a highly popular laugh-evoker for two centuries. This is largely due to the change of attitudes of very many white Americans influenced by the civil rights movement. Nor do Negroes make fun of themselves publicly. Another more subtle factor may be the avoidance of jocularity by both Negroes and whites due to the tense and explosive racial situation.

In the United States, also largely since World War II, jokes about Jews—the perennial scapegoats—have vanished. An undying outrage at the diabolical anti-Semitic practices of the Germans has created new positive attitudes among many toward Jews. Extremely important, second and later generations of American Jews have achieved general and specific positions of distinction in American life. A disproportionate number of them, in comparison with other ethnic stocks, according to studies of stratification, are now rated as middle class or above. They serve as distinguished members of Congress, judges of all levels, and state and local officials—both appointive and elective positions. They are to be found in exceptional numbers in the professions, particularly law, teaching, medicine, and science, and in American economic life, especially retail trade and banking. They are not butts of laugher any more. At the same time they are leaders in our amusement industry and provide us with some of our most eminent comedians.

Other situational changes have affected the volume of laughter. There seems to be less laughter of sympathy and empathy, less laughter of comradeship and compassion, less laughter about human indiscretions and failings (for example, drunkenness).

G. Laughter is becoming more restrained. In frontier days and while we were predominantly a rural, village, and small-city people, we as persons had fewer contacts in an average day or week; but contacts were closer, freer, and more open than they are for most people today. This made for a greater reciprocity and mutuality of emotion and feeling, which in turn created a more favorable climate for laughter in the group. Today people tend to be more passive and reserved with respect to each other. Many seem to go to great lengths to disguise their feelings, both positive and negative, from others (and possibly even from themselves). Also the different sociocultural segments of the country are too busy taking themselves seriously, and too busy pushing, grabbing, elbowing, outdoing, chasing around, and climbing to join wholeheartedly with each other in widespread common laughter. While we have much leisure for most people in modern society, probably more than in any time in the past, it does not seem to stir the jocund mood as it has been thought to do in the past.

The group laughter that we do have is not the rambunctious, raucous, boot-banging, hat-swinging, gutty ya-hooing of the frontier gathering: the county fair, the barnraising, the husking bee, the Saturday-afternoon assembly on the porch of the village general store. It seem to be less and less noisy and rollicking, and more and more sedate, decorous, and tempered or cramped. Loud laughter, long prohibited by polite society's code of proprieties, seems to be increasingly tabooed among all population elements.

It also seems likely that there is less laughter in the sense of the physico-psychic act with its convulsive movements of the diaphragm and its spasmodic expulsions of breath, and more smiling in place of it. The smile expresses the more restricted impulsive state of the individual of today in humorous situations, gives him satisfying release, whether alone or with others, makes his expression less public, and at the same time enables him, often subtly and pointedly, to communicate amusement, friendliness, approval, derision, contempt or hatred.

H. There seems to be some shifting of attention to less humorous themes on the part of some of the mass media providing amusement. This is especially true of the comic strips, probably the most widely consumed and widely influential of all the laugh media in the United States. A most comprehensive survey conducted by the Communication Research Center of Boston University during January, 1962, indicated that the comics at that time were read by more than one hundred million Americans any Sunday or weekday in the year. This means that the comics enjoy a higher readership on the whole than any other feature in the newspaper, with the exception of front-page headlines (White & Wells, 3). Originally intended for children, they now draw a very wide, almost universal, public. They appeal to all classes and areas of our society, because they are a response to the folklore and reflect the widespread concerns of the folk as a whole. Most of them have sought to portray from day to day, in a humorous, human way the things that are occupying the daily attention and interest of a very large number of people.

The comics still are intended to amuse people, but a dwindling away of their humor and comic element—their devotion to fun-making—seems to be evident. This appears especially in the shifting of attention to less humorous themes. The old standbys—the clever and droll acts of children, the Mr. and Mrs. conflict and intrigue, the pratfalls and horseplay, the human antics of animals—still are used, and still inspire laughter; but most the "comics" have as their basic areas of interest fantasy, science fiction, suspense and horror, social commentary, adventure, fairy tales, nature facts, and, recently, Bible stories (e.g., the strip "Tales from the Great Book"). These themes do not induce laughter, nor are they intended to do so. The very decline in humor-eliciting themes among these reflectors of popular interest and mood seems to indicate less interest in humor and laughter, and at least implies a corresponding diminution of laughter.

I. A consideration of special importance is the diminishing and less happy laughter of a fearsome and insecure people. There is a great likelihood that humor has decayed, and that laughter in general has diminished and become less happy during the present century, especially since World War II. If this is true it can be attributed in large measure to the tremendously dangerous social crises and changes that the people have been subjected to.

The interlocking world has had two ghastly world wars, several dozen lesser wars, and continued threats of wars; the protracted cold war; the pervading threat of the sudden annihilation of millions upon millions of people and the devastation of millions of square miles of the earth's surface and all on it by thermonuclear missiles; the encroaching asphyxiation by the polluted atmosphere and poisoning by polluted water; the ominous increase of world population and the continuous threat of starvation for much of the world; the bitter and almost universal racial and ethnic strife; the struggle between political factions and between social classes; the acute gap between the generations; the birth throes and growing pains of, and rivalries among, dozens of new nations; the moral confusion; and the anarchy of groups. Such conditions have created among many a state of fear, insecurity, despair, and unhappiness. Such a state in turn is a potent enemy of happy humor and a blanket on happy laughter. Fear especially is an underlying feeling motivating the young. One often hears that young folks do not seem to laugh as much as their grandparents did.

This situation has a conformist response as one of its noteworthy aspects. When people are fearsome, lack confidence, and feel inscure, they stress uniformity and conformism. They feel safer and stronger when all accept the same values, say the same things, nourish the same hopes, embrace the same social philosophy, display the same intolerances and antipathies, and exercise a herdlike uniformity of behavior and a herdlike resistance to any deviation from group unity and uniformity (Muggeridge, 61). For them their common conformism is a kind of protective huddling.

Humor and laughter, however, need freedom; without it they cannot exist. They rest upon unconstrained and accepted divergence and contrast and independence of interest, belief, and action; upon unhampered objectivity and permissive creativeness. They also flourish in a group or society in which a spirit of confidence and tolerance pevails, and in which criticism can be freely engaged in. What is of special point here is that many social laughter-inducing situations are in large measure breaches of conformity norms. But where and when conformism is a fetish, nonconformist attitudes and behaviors are looked at askance. Hence the humorist strikes a discordant note in a conformist society; he advertises deviance from herd ways, and this deviance in its very nature constitutes criticism and subversion. The laughter he inspires is itself a form of insurgency.

In the United States today we have a widespread popularity of conformisms and subordination to their dictates. Most people are careful to abide by the highly touted values and behavioral norms and forms of their main peer and/or reference groups, or their cliques, or their social class, and in many instances of the mass society. Indeed, as we conform to the dictates of the various establishments of which we are members we seem to suffer a procession complex—a disposition to be part of a column of marching creatures, to engage in a tribal cadence. But this means that many viewpoints and things and acts not in accord with the relevant reigning conventions should be shunned as laughable matters. Furthermore, the lockstep of the procession certainly is not laughable to the participants but only to the minority of irreverent observers.

Another signal aspect of this smothering conformance is the surmise that there has been a marked decline in laughter expressing dissent, opposition, or controversy. Dudden (34-36) has contended that political humor and its laughter—laughing at politicians, political parties, political ideas, political tactics in general, and the ideas, organizations, and tactics of political dissenters in particular—which has been a characteristic of the people of the United States, has markedly declined in the last few decades; and he attributes it in considerable part to the increasing conformism. Harris (13) stated that "in recent years in America, politicians have been advised—and for the most part have taken the advice—to avoid wit, especially on controversial subjects." There also seems to be a tendency among television sponsors to avoid having anything politically controversial in their programs. Wit seems to be avoided in radio and television newscasts.[9]

Related to the diminished quantity of laughter in our world

---

[9] On the relation of laughter and conformism see Bier, 28-29; Dudden, 19-20, 22-23, 34-36; Harris, 13-19; Muggeridge.

is the change in its quality: there seems to be so much less of happy laughter. Happy laughter here is not to be confused with the hysterical laughter of those who view a revved-up television comedy. This ". . . denatured humor is calculated to take the audience's mind off its troubles, anesthetize its critical intelligence with stultifying merriment, and thus decrease its sales resistance (Carlisle, xiii). What we have in mind is the possibility, even the actuality, of a change in the emotional quality and the spirit of much laughter, namely that there is less of the evanescent laughter of happiness: of joy, gaiety, contentment, rejoicing, and free-wheeling, free-ranging fun-making. This, if it is true, may be due to the fact that among very many people in the modern world there is vastly more weariness and seriousness and skepticism, and less real happiness. There is less laughter as a positive act of "joyous surrender" (Gregory, 96).

An indicator of marked significance of this decline of happy laughter is the prevalence and popularity, not only in the United States but in the Western world, of "black" and "sick" humor—humor which produces negativistic laughter. This humor is antithetical, anti-climactic, disaffected with an disabused about everything, bitter and grim, sneering, deflationary of persons and conditions, of social life in general in most of its features. If there is some difference of stress, black humor is an expression of dark rage at miserable conditions or values or trends, while sick humor is a perverse enjoyment of the same, a psychopathological stance close to sado-masochism.[10] This humor quite definitely seems to be an expression of terror, of tension, of defeat, a reflection of social malaise. It permeates much of our cartooning, the comics, popular music, current poetry, novels, and movies, much of our joking. It is directed against such aspects of our social life as overtolerance, intolerance, opinion-engineering, national self-righteousness, commercialized religion, "culture," the euphemisms and hypocrisies of both the masses and the classes. It it the adverse humor that elicits the hysterical accusatory laugh, the

---

[10] This distinction from Bier, 294-295.

snigger of contempt, the sardonic smile.[11] Geared to such humor, we have the laughter of bitterness and cynicism in place of the laughter of joyousness.

4. THE PRESENT NEED FOR POSITIVE LAUGHTER

The disturbed state of the nation and the world indicates the need for robust, healthy humor and joyous, positive laughter. Laughter, as has been noted repeatedly, is a many-sided human response to social conditions and a highly versatile and influential social agent.

There is a vast reservoir of laughter that is socially positive; and it is made up of laughters that have great alleviative, restorative, and constructive capability and effect. If these positive, beneficial laughters can be evoked, maintained, and spread in increasing volume and variety among contemporary men, they, in the light of their demonstrated historical uses and effects, have vast promise as means of countering, even correcting, many of the sinister conditions, trends, and forces of our present complex, interlocking, and chaotic world. Especially is positive humor and laughter necessary in stemming the tide of fear, insecurity, dullness, passivity, apathy, cycnicism, misanthropy, bitterness, "sickness," despair, horrible uniformity, unutterable boredom.

It is of special moment that the beneficial laughters can be positively controlled; that is, they can be originated and manipulated as to both kind and amount by social managers committed to positive social objectives. This can be done in order to suggest and encourage desirable social ends, and to stimulate personal and group energy in socially wholesome directions.[12]

Many vital, healthful, beneficial laughters are available. They constitute a social resource of inestimable value and potentiality, but thus far of limited telic utilization. Conspicuous among such

---

[11] On black-sick humor see Bier, 293-301; De Mott.

[12] This deliberate attempt to induce and maintain laughter for socially positive or constructive purposes and ends can be looked upon as the positive social control of laughter, as against the negative social restraints imposed upon laughter to control or prevent unconventional or anti-social effects (chap. xv).

laughters are the laughter of joy, of high spirits and of cheer, which drowns out or enables the actors to laugh off worry, the feeling of fear, the attitudes of bitterness and despair, the feeling of defeat; the laughter of free expression of the sense of liberty and the related feeling of freedom from social constraint, pressure, rigidity, and repression; the mirthful laughter that heightens the group tone and restores the equilibrium of persons; the laughter of amusement at human foibles and follies; the laughter of kindly criticism and challenge; the laughter which is provoked by the discrepancy between what is and what ought to be, and which assists in a rational and well-balanced evaluation of the world, and stimulates correction; the optimistic laughter which expresses hope, exalts human aspiration, and exults in achievement; the laughter of triumph over adversity; the playful laughter which averts or bridges or heals social breaches by thwarting or diverting the antagonistically inclined, and cajoling associates out of attitudes of stubbornness and hostility; the laughter (or smile) of recognition of others, of friendly greeting, of affection, of sympathy, of consolation, of concern for others in their misfortunes and sorrows; the laughter awakened to reward socially beneficent achievements: the laughter of approval and applause.

Such laughters are essential to the sanity, dignity, happiness, humanity—the very survival—of man. They cannot be allowed to perish from the earth. And when we—ranging from us as individuals in everyday association with our fellows to our public humorists and comedians—come to employ our vast battery of media to induce these laughters on a large scale, we may vastly enhance human well-being on the earth. As Armstrong (73) put it more than four decades ago: "If we could laugh more collectively, if we could laugh municipally, regionally, internationally, what might not the force of laughter achieve."

BIBLIOGRAPHY

Allport, Floyd H., Social Psychology. Boston: Houghton Mifflin, 1924. "Laughter," 252-258.

Allport, Gordon W., The Person in Psychology. Boston: Beacon Press, 1968. 76, 134.

Armstrong, Martin, Laughing: An Essay. New York: Harper, 1928.

Barron, Milton L., "A Content Analysis of Intergroup Humor," American Sociological Review, 15 (Feb., 1950): 88-94.

Beard, Charles A. & Mary R., The Rise of American Civilization. New York: Macmillan, 1934. 2 vols.

Beatty, Jerome, Jr., "Humor vs. Taboo: The Sorrowful Story of the Cartoon." Saturday Review, 40 (Nov. 23, 1957): 11-15.

Bergson, Henri, Laughter: An Essay on the Meaning of the Comic. (Trans. by Cloudsley Brereton & Fred Rothwell.) New York: Macmillan, 1911.

Berlyne, D. E., "Laughter, Humor, and Play," in Gardner Lindzey & Elliott Aronson, eds., The Handbook of Social Psychology, 2nd ed. Reading, Mass.: Addison-Wesley, 1969. III, 795-852 (humor and laughter portion of chap., 795-813).

Bier, Jesse, The Rise and Fall of American Humor. New York: Holt, Rinehart & Winston, 1968.

Blair, Walter, Native American Humor (1800-1900). New York: American Book, 1937.

Blau, Peter M., The Dynamics of Bureaucracy. Chicago: Univ. of Chicago Press, 1955. 91-95.

Bogardus, Emory S., Fundamentals of Social Psychology. New York: Century, 1924. 69-74.

Bradney, Pamela, "The Joking Relationship in Industry," Human Relations, 19 (No. 2, 1957): 179-187.

Breed, Warren, "Mass Communication and Socio-Cultural Structure," Social Forces, 37 (Dec., 1958): 109-116.

Burma, John H., "Humor as a Technique in Race Conflict," American Sociological Review, 11 (Dec., 1946): 716-715.

Burns, Tom, "Friends, Enemies, and the Polite Fiction," American Sociological Review, 18 (Dec., 1953): 654-662.

Cameron, William B., "The Sociology of Humor and Vice Versa," in his Informal Sociology: A Casual Introduction to Sociological Thinking. New York: Random House, Inc., 1963. 79-94.

Carlisle, Henry C., Jr., ed., American Satire: In Prose and Verse. New York: Random House, Inc., 1962. xiii-xvii.

Carlyle, Thomas, Sartor Resartus (orig. pub. 1833-34), Archibald MacMeachan, ed. Boston: Ginn, 1896. Book 1, chap. 4; also 298.

Coser, Rose Laub, "Some Social Functions of Laughter: A Study of Humor in a Hospital Setting," Human Relations, 12 (No. 2, 1959): 171-182.
———"Laughter Among Colleagues: A Study of Social Functions of Humor Among the Staff of a Mental Hospital," Psychiatry, 23 (Feb., 1960): 81-95.
———"Role Distance, Sociological Ambivalence, and Transitional Status Systems," American Journal of Sociology, 72 (Sept., 1966): 173-187.

Daniels, Arlene K. & Richard R., "The Social Function of the Career Fool," Psychiatry, 27 (Aug., 1964): 219-229.

Darwin, Charles Robert, The Expression of the Emotions in Man and Animals, New York: Appleton, 1873. 198-212.

Davis, Harold T., The Fine Art of Punning. Evanston, Ill.: Principia Press of Illinois, 1954.

De Mott, Benjamin, "The New Irony: Sicknicks and Others," American Scholar, 31 (Winter, 1961-62): 108-119.

Dexter, Lewis A. & David Manning White, eds., People, Society, and Mass Communications. New York: Free Press of Glencoe, 1964.

Dudden, Arthur P., "Introduction" to Arthur P. Dudden, ed., Assault of Laughter: A Treasury of American Political Humor. New York: Thomas Yoseloff, 1962. 19-37.

Duncan, Hugh D., Language and Literature in Society. Chicago: Univ. of Chicago Press, 1953, 49-57.

——Communication and Social Order. New York: Bedminster Press, 1962. 330-331, 376-380, 387-390.

Eastman, Max, The Sense of Humor. New York: Scribner's Sons, 1922.

——Enjoyment of Laughter, New York: Simon & Schuster, 1936.

Elliott, Robert C., The Power of Satire, Magic, Ritual, Art. Princeton, N.J.: Princeton Univ. Press, 1960. 49-99, 257-275.

Esar, Evan, The Humor of Humor. New York: Horizon Press, Inc., 1952.

Eysenck, H. J., "National Differences in 'Sense of Humor': Three Experimental and Statistical Studies," Character & Personality, 13 (Sept., 1944): 37-54.

——"National Differences in Humor," American Mercury, 61 (Sept., 1943): 332-337.

Flugel, J. C., "Humor and Laughter," in Gardner Lindzey, ed., Handbook of Social Psychology. Cambridge, Mass.: Addison-Wesley Pub., 1954. II, 709-734.

Freud, Sigmund, Wit and Its Relation to the Unconscious. (Transl. and Int. by A. A. Britt). New York: Moffat, Yard, 1916.

Fry, William F., Jr., Sweet Madness: A Study of Humor. Palo Alto, Cal.: Pacific Books, 1963.

Girsdansky, Michael, The Adventure of Language. Englewood Cliffs, N.J.: Prentice-Hall, 1960.

Goodchilds, Jacqueline, "Effects of Being Witty on Position in the Social Structure of a Small Group," Sociometry, 22 (Sept., 1959): 261-272.

Goodchilds, Jacqueline & Evart E. Smith, "The Wit and His Group," Human Relations, 17 (Feb., 1964): 23-31.

Grant, Mary A., The Ancient Rhetorical Theories of the Laughable: The Greek Rhetoricians and Cicero. (University of Wisconsin Studies in Language and Literature, No. 21.) Madison, Wis.: Univ. of Wisconsin Press, 1924.

Gregory, J. C., The Nature of Laughter. London: Kegan Paul, Trench, Trubner, 1924. Espec. 1-40, 66-99.

Grieg, John Y. T., The Psychology of Laughter and Comedy. New York: Dodd, Mead, 1923.

Grotjahn, Martin, Beyond Laughter. New York: Blakiston Div., McGraw-Hill, 1957.

Hall, Wade, The Smiling Phoenix: Southern Humor from 1865 to 1914. Gainesville, Fla.: Univ. of Florida Press, 1965.

Hanser, Richard, "Wit as a Weapon," Saturday Review, 35 (Nov. 8, 1952): 13-14, 51.

Harris, Leon A., The Fine Art of Political Wit. New York: Dutton, 1964.

Hayworth, Donald, "The Social Origin and Function of Laughter," Psychological Review, 35 (Sept., 1928): 367-384.

Hazlitt, W. Carew, Studies in Jocular Literature. London: Elliott Stock, 1890.

Homans, George C., The Human Group. New York: Harcourt, Brace, 1950.

Johnson, Gerald W., "Laugh, Casca, Laugh." Saturday Review, 50 (Dec. 2, 1967): 16-19.

Kambouropoulou, Polyxenie, "Individual Differences in the Sense of Humor and Their Relation to Temperamental Differences," Archives of Psychology. New York: Columbia University. No. 121, Vol. 130, pp. 5-83.

Kimmins, C. W., The Springs of Laughter. London: Methuen, 1928.

Klapp, Orrin E., "The Fool as a Social Type," American Journal of Sociology, 53 (Sept., 1949): 157-162.
——Heroes, Villains, and Fools. New York: Prentice-Hall, 1962. 68-91.

Koestler, Arthur, Insight and Outlook. New York: Macmillan, 1949. 3-110.

Kronenberger, Louis, The Thread of Laughter. New York: Knopf, 1952. 3-11.

Kronenberger, Louis, ed., Cavalcade of Comedy. New York: Simon & Schuster, 1953. xi-xv.

Landis, Carney & John W. H. Ross, "Humor and Its Relation to

Other Personality Traits," Journal of Social Psychology, 4 (May, 1935): 156-175.

Langer, Susanne, "The Comic Rhythm," in Robert W. Corrigan, ed., Comedy: Meaning and Form. San Francisco: Chandler, 1965. 119-140.

Leacock, Stephen E., Humor: Its Theory and Technique. New York: Dodd, Mead, 1935.

Legman, Gershon, "Toward a Motif-Index of Erotic Humor," Journal of American Folklore, 75 (July, 1862): 227-248.

Lumley, Frederick E., Means of Social Control. New York: Century, 1925. "Satire," 237-259; "Laughter," 260-287.

MacDougall, Curtis D., Understanding Public Opinion. New York: Macmillan, 1952. "Wit and Humor," 426-434.

McDougall, William, Outline of Psychology, New York: Scribner's Sons, 1923. "A Theory of Laughter," 165-170.

Martindale, Don, American Social Structure: Historical Antecedents and Contemporary Analyses. New York: Appleton-Century-Crofts, 1960. viii-ix, 3-27.

————Community Character and Civilization. New York: Free Press of Glencoe, 1963. 193-194.

Masson, Thomas L., Our American Humorists. Freeport, N.Y.: Books for Libraries Press, 1966.

Mechanic, D., Students Under Stress. New York: Free Press of Glencoe, 1962. 50-51, 125-127, 142, 144, 172.

Menon, V. K. Krishna, A Theory of Laughter, London: George Allen & Unwin, 1931.

Meredith, George, An Essay on Comedy (int. & ed., Wylie Sypher). Garden City, N.Y.: Doubleday, 1956. (Orig. pub. 1877.)

Middleton, Russell, "Negro and White Reactions to Racial Humor." Sociometry, 22 (June, 1959): 175-183.

Middleton, Russell & John Moland, "Humor in Negro and White Subcultures: A Study of Jokes among University Students." American Sociological Review, 24 (Feb., 1959): 61-69.

Mikes, George, Eight Humorists. London: Allen-Wingate, 1954.

Monro, D. H., Argument of Laughter. Melbourne: Melbourne Univ. Press, 1951.

Montagu, Ashley, "Why Man Laughs," Think, 26 (Apr., 1960): 30-32.

———The Anatomy of Swearing. New York: Macmillan, 1967. 78-84.

Muggeridge, Malcolm, "America Needs a Punch," Esquire, 49 (Apr., 1958): 59-61.

Murray, H. A., Jr., "The Psychology of Humor," Journal of Abnormal and Social Psychology, 29 (Apr.-June, 1934): 66-81.

Myers, Henry A., "The Analysis of Laughter," Sewanee Review, 43 (Oct.-Dec., 1935): 452-463.

Myrdal, Gunnar, An American Dilemma. New York: Harper, 1944. 38-39, 160-161.

Obrdlik, Antonin J., "Gallows Humor—A Sociological Phenomenon," American Journal of Sociology, 47 (Mar., 1942): 709-716.

Oleson, Virginia & Alvi Waik Whittacker, "Adjudication of Student Awareness in Professional Socialization: The Language of Laughter and Silences," Sociological Quarterly, 7 (Summer, 1966): 381-396.

Omwake, Louise, "Factors Influencing the Sense of Humor." Journal of Social Psychology, 10 (Feb., 1939): 95-104.

Patrick, George T. W., The Psychology of Relaxation. Boston: Houghton Mifflin, 1916. "The Psychology of Laughter," 99-142.

Piddington, Ralph, The Psychology of Laughter: A Study in Social Adaptation (2nd ed.). New York: Gamut Press, 1962.

Radcliffe-Brown, A. R., Structure and Function in Primitive Society. London: Cohen & West, 1952. "On Joking Relationships," 90-104; "A Further Note on Joking Relationships," 105-116.

Rapp, Albert, "Toward an Eclectic and Multilateral Theory of Laughter and Humor," Journal of General Psychology, 26 (Apr., 1947): 207-219.

———"A Phylogenetic Theory of Wit and Humor," Journal of Social Psychology, 30 (Aug., 1949): 81-96.

———The Origins of Wit and Humor. New York: Dutton, 1951.

Rinder, Irwin D., "A Note on Humor as an Index of Minority Group Morale." Phylon, 26 (Summer, 1965): 117-121.

Rosenberg, Bernard & Gilbert Shapiro, "Marginality of Jewish Humor," Midstream, 4 (Spring, 1959): 70-80.

Rourke, Constance M., American Humor: A Study of the National Character. New York: Harcourt, Brace, 1931.

Rovit, Earl, "Jewish Humor in American Life," American Scholar, 36 (Spring, 1967): 237-245.

Schulman, Max, American Humor: Its Cause and Cure, Yale Review, 51 (Oct., 1961): 119-124.

Seward, Samuel S., Jr., The Paradox of the Ludicrous. Stanford, Cal.: Stanford Univ. Press, 1930.

Sidis, Boris, The Psychology of Laughter. New York: Appleton, 1913.

Smith, Nathalie V. & W. Edgar Vinacke, "Reactions to Humorous Stimuli of Different Generations of Japanese, Chinese, and Caucasians in Hawaii," Journal of Social Psychology, 34 (Aug., 1951): 69-96.

Smith, Willard, The Nature of Comedy. Boston: Richard G. Badger, 1930.

Stephenson, Richard M., "Conflict and Control Functions of Humor," American Journal of Sociology, 56 (May, 1951): 569-574.

Sterling, Philip, "A Meaning of Laughter," in Philip Sterling, ed., Laughing on the Outside: The Intelligent White Reader's Guide to Negro Tales and Humor. New York: Grosset & Dunlap, 1965. 17-19, 21-25.

Stylites, Simon, "Humor and Religion," I and II, Christian Century, 77 (Feb. 17, 1960): 207; 77 (Feb. 24, 1960): 239.

Sully, James, An Essay on Laughter: Its Forms, Its Causes, Its Development, and Its Values. New York: Longmans, Green, 1902.

Swabey, Marie Collins, Comic Laughter: A Philosophical Essay. New Haven, Conn.: Yale Univ. Press, 1961.

Tandy, Jennette, Crackerbox Philosophers in American Humor and Satire. New York: Columbia Univ. Press, 1925.

Thomson, Donald F., "The Joking Relationship and Organized

Obscenity in North Queensland," American Anthropologist, 37 (July-Sept., 1935): 460-490.

Thorp, Willard, American Humorists. Minneapolis: Univ. of Minnesota Press, 1964.

Torrance, E. Paul, Constructive Behavior: Stress, Personality, and Mental Health. Belmont, Cal.: Wadsworth, 1965.

Wallis, Wilson D., "Why Do We Laugh?" Scientific Monthly 15 (1922): 343-347.

Warner, W. Lloyd, The Living and the Dead. New Haven, Conn.: Yale Univ. Press, 1959.

Weber, Brom, ed., An Anthology of American Humor. New York: Crowell, 1962.

White, David Manning & Robert H. Wells, eds., The Funnies: An American Idiom. New York: Free Press, 1963.

Willmann, John M., "An Analysis of Humor and Laughter," American Journal of Psychology, 53 (Jan., 1940): 70-85.

Winick, Charles, "Space Jokes as Indication of Attitudes Toward Space," Journal of Social Issues, 17 (No. 2, 1961): 43-49.
———"Teen-agers, Satire, and *Mad*," in Lewis A. Dexter & David Manning White, eds., People, Society, and Mass Communications. New York: Free Press of Glencoe, 1964. 263-282.

Wolff, H. A., C. E. Smith, & H. A. Murray, "The Psychology of Humor: 1. A Study of Responses to Race-Disparagement Jokes," Journal of Abnormal & Social Psychology, 28 (Jan.-Mar., 1934): 341-365.

Worcester, David, The Art of Satire. Cambridge, Mass.: Harvard Univ. Press, 1940. 8-9, 16, 34-37.

Yates, Morris W., The American Humorist: Conscience of the Twentieth Century. Ames, Iowa: Iowa State Univ. Press, 1964.

Zijderveld, Anton J., "Jokes and Their Relationship to Social Reality." Social Research, 35 (Summer, 1968): 286-311.

INDEX